3 ingredient cookbook

D0576440

Brie Bites

1 package (17½ ounces) frozen puff pastry, thawed
¼ cup apricot preserves or red pepper jelly
1 (5-inch) brie round, cut into 32 chunks

1. Preheat oven to 400°F. Cut each puff pastry sheet into 16 squares.

2. Spread ½ teaspoon apricot preserves on each square. Place chunk of brie on one side of square, fold over opposite edge, use tines of fork to seal completely. Place 1 inch apart on ungreased baking sheets.

3. Bake 10 to 13 minutes or until pastry is light golden brown.

Makes 32 appetizers

Simple Salsa Roll-ups

1 package (8 ounces) cream cheese, softened
1 cup salsa
4 (8-inch) flour tortillas

Combine cream cheese and salsa in medium bowl; mix well. Spread thin layer on each tortilla. Roll up tortillas; cut each roll-up into 4 individual spirals.

Makes 16 appetizers

Table of Contents

Original Ranch® Drummettes

**1 packet (1 ounce) HIDDEN VALLEY® The Original Ranch®
Salad Dressing & Seasoning Mix**
¼ cup vegetable oil
24 chicken drummettes (about 2 pounds)

Combine dressing mix and oil in large bowl. Add drummettes; toss
well to coat. Arrange on rack placed in foil-lined baking pan; bake at
425°F for 25 minutes. Turn drummettes over; bake additional
20 minutes.

Makes 24 drummettes

Spicy Hot Variation: Add 2 tablespoons red pepper sauce to dressing
mixture before coating.

Serving Suggestion: Dip cooked drummettes in prepared Hidden
Valley® Original Ranch® salad dressing.

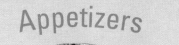

Bandito Buffalo Wings

1 package (1.25 ounces) ORTEGA® Taco Seasoning Mix
12 (about 1 pound *total*) chicken wings
   ORTEGA Salsa (any flavor)

PREHEAT oven to 375°F. Lightly grease 13×9-inch baking pan.

PLACE seasoning mix in heavy-duty plastic or paper bag. Add
3 chicken wings; shake well to coat. Place wings in prepared pan.
Repeat until all wings have been coated.

BAKE for 35 to 40 minutes or until juices run clear. Serve with salsa
for dipping.   *Makes 6 appetizer servings*

tip

Chicken wings are always a favorite party
food. Plan on 2 wings per person for an
appetizer and about 6 for a main course.

Bandito Buffalo Wings

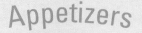

Valentine Pizzas

1 package (12 ounces) refrigerated flaky buttermilk biscuits (10 biscuits)
1 cup RAGÚ® Organic Pasta Sauce
1 package (8 ounces) shredded mozzarella cheese

Preheat oven to 375°.

Separate each biscuit into 2 rounds. Shape each round into an oval. On ungreased baking sheet, use 2 ovals to create a heart shape by slightly over lapping and pulling end to make the point. Repeat with remaining rounds. Evenly top each with Pasta Sauce, then cheese.

Bake 10 minutes or until golden. Garnish, if desired, with heart shaped pepperoni slices and sliced pitted ripe olives to create X's and O's. *Makes 10 servings*

Prep Time: 10 minutes
Cook Time: 10 minutes

Italian Pita Chips

½ cup (1 stick) butter, melted
1 packet Italian dressing mix
4 pita rounds, split in half

1. Preheat oven to 300°F. Spray baking sheet with nonstick cooking spray.

2. Combine butter and dressing mix in small bowl. Brush mixture over pita bread halves and place on prepared baking sheet. Bake about 20 minutes or until crispy.

3. Carefully break into pieces. Serve with your favorite dip or spread.

Makes 4 appetizer servings

Cocktail Bites

1¼ cups red currant jelly or cranberry sauce
1¼ cups ketchup
2 pounds HILLSHIRE FARM® Lit'l Smokies

Heat jelly and ketchup in small saucepan over medium heat *or* microwave, uncovered, at HIGH 1 to 2 minutes or until mixture blends smoothly. Add Lit'l Smokies; cook until links are hot. Serve with frilled toothpicks. *Makes about 100 hors d'oeuvres*

Vegetable Cream Cheese

**1 envelope LIPTON® RECIPE SECRETS® Vegetable
Soup Mix**
2 packages (8 ounces each) cream cheese, softened
2 tablespoons milk

1. In medium bowl, combine all ingredients; chill 2 hours.

2. Serve on bagels or with assorted fresh vegetables.

Makes 2½ cups spread

Prep Time: 10 minutes
Chill Time: 2 hours

Stuffed Bundles

1 package (10 ounces) refrigerated pizza dough
2 ounces lean ham or turkey ham, chopped
½ cup (2 ounces) shredded sharp Cheddar cheese

1. Preheat oven to 425°F. Coat 12 standard (2½-inch) muffin pan
cups with nonstick cooking spray.

2. Unroll dough on flat surface; cut into 12 pieces, (4×3-inch
rectangles). Divide ham and cheese between dough rectangles. Bring
corners of dough together, pinching to seal. Place, smooth side up, in
prepared muffin cups.

3. Bake 10 to 12 minutes or until golden. *Makes 12 servings*

Pizza Stuffed Cherry Tomatoes

1 bag (20 ounces) vine ripened cherry tomatoes (about 20)
¼ cup shredded mozzarella cheese
20 slices pepperoni

1. Preheat broiler. Using a paring knife, slice upper ⅛ inch off stem end of tomatoes, keeping tops and bottom pieces next to each other. Seed and core tomatoes using a small melon baller or by carefully pinching out core using thumb and index finger.

2. To assemble, fill each tomato to the brim with cheese, top with a slice of pepperoni, and cover with tomato top. Secure with a toothpick.

3. Place filled tomatoes on baking sheet and broil on top oven rack, about 6 inches from heat source, 3 minutes, until cheese is melted and tomatoes just begin to shrivel.

4. Transfer tomatoes to paper towel-lined plate to drain. Remove toothpicks before serving small children. Serve warm, not hot.

Makes about 20 appetizers

Pizza Stuffed Cherry Tomatoes

Baked Brie

½ pound Brie cheese, rind removed
¼ cup chopped pecans
¼ cup KARO® Dark Corn Syrup

1. Preheat oven to 350°F. Place cheese in shallow oven-safe serving dish. Top with pecans and corn syrup.

2. Bake 8 to 10 minutes or until cheese is almost melted. Serve warm with plain crackers or melba toast.   *Makes 8 servings*

Prep Time: 3 minutes
Cook Time: 10 minutes

tip

Brie is a soft cheese with an edible white rind and a creamy interior. Its flavor is mild and is delicious whether eaten cold or warm.

Bacon-Wrapped Breadsticks

8 slices bacon
16 garlic-flavored breadsticks (about 8 inches long)
¾ cup grated Parmesan cheese

1. Cut bacon slices in half lengthwise. Wrap half slice of bacon diagonally around each breadstick. Combine Parmesan cheese and 2 tablespoons chopped fresh parsley, if desired, in shallow dish; set aside.

2. Place 4 breadsticks on double layer of paper towels in microwave oven. Microwave on HIGH 2 to 3 minutes or until bacon is cooked through. Immediately roll breadsticks in Parmesan mixture to coat. Repeat with remaining breadsticks. *Makes 16 breadsticks*

Cherry Tomato Pops

4 (1-ounce each) mozzarella cheese sticks
8 cherry tomatoes
3 tablespoons ranch dressing

1. Slice string cheese in half lengthwise. Trim stem end of each cherry tomato and gently squeeze out about ¼ teaspoon of pulp and seeds.

2. Press end of string cheese into hollowed tomato to make cherry tomato pop. Serve with ranch dressing as dip. *Makes 8 pops*

Honey Nut Brie

¼ cup honey
¼ cup coarsely chopped pecans
1 tablespoon brandy (optional)
1 wheel (14 ounces) Brie cheese (about 5-inch diameter)

1. Preheat oven to 500°F. Combine honey, pecans and brandy, if desired, in small bowl. Place cheese on large round ovenproof platter or in 9-inch pie plate.

2. Bake 4 to 5 minutes or until cheese softens. Drizzle honey mixture over top of cheese. Bake 2 to 3 minutes longer or until topping is thoroughly heated. *Do not melt cheese.* *Makes 16 to 20 servings*

Tip: Serve this party dish with crackers, tart apple wedges and seedless grapes.

Main Dishes

1-2-3 Chili

2 pounds ground beef
4 cans (8 ounces each) tomato sauce
3 cans (15½ ounces each) chili beans in mild or spicy
sauce, undrained

SLOW COOKER DIRECTIONS

1. Brown beef in large nonstick skillet over medium-high heat, stirring to break up meat. Drain fat. Combine beef, tomato sauce and beans with sauce in slow cooker; mix well.

2. Cover; cook on LOW 6 to 8 hours.

3. Serve with shredded Cheddar cheese and sliced green onions, if desired. *Makes 8 servings*

Tip: Just dump everything into your slow cooker. Set it up before work and come home to a batch of delicious chili! It tastes great with cornbread, too.

3 ingredient cookbook

Hot & Sour Chicken

4 to 6 boneless skinless chicken breasts (about 1 to 1½ pounds)
1 cup chicken or vegetable broth
1 package (1 ounce) dry hot-and-sour soup mix

SLOW COOKER DIRECTIONS

Place chicken in slow cooker. Add broth and soup mix. Cover; cook on LOW 5 to 6 hours. Garnish as desired.   *Makes 4 to 6 servings*

Meal Idea: Serve this dish over a bed of snow peas and sugar snap peas tossed with diced red bell pepper.

Sloppy Joes On Buns

2 pounds ground beef
1 medium onion, chopped (optional)
1 jar (1 pound 10 ounces) RAGÚ® Organic Pasta Sauce
8 hamburger buns

In 12-inch nonstick skillet, brown ground beef with onion; drain. Stir in Pasta Sauce. Bring to a boil over high heat. Reduce heat to medium and simmer covered, stirring occasionally, 10 minutes. Serve on buns.   *Makes 8 servings*

Prep Time: 5 minutes
Cook Time: 15 minutes

Hot & Sour Chicken

Cranberry-Onion Pork Roast

1 boneless pork loin roast (about 2 pounds)
1 can (16 ounces) whole cranberry sauce
1 package (1 ounce) dry onion soup mix

Season roast with salt and pepper; place over indirect heat on grill. Stir together cranberry sauce and onion soup mix in small microwavable bowl. Heat, covered, in microwave until hot, about 1 minute. Baste roast with cranberry mixture every 10 minutes until roast is done (internal temperature with a meat thermometer is 155° to 160°F), about 30 to 45 minutes. Let roast rest about 5 to 8 minutes before slicing to serve. Heat any leftover basting mixture to boiling; stir and boil for 5 minutes. Serve alongside roast.

Makes 4 to 6 servings

Favorite recipe from *National Pork Board*

tip

Lean cuts of pork, like the loin roast, are terrific sources of protein, B vitamins and zinc. They also adapt well to a wide variety of flavors and cooking methods.

Cranberry-Onion Pork Roast

BBQ Roast Beef

2 pounds boneless cooked roast beef
1 bottle (12 ounces) barbecue sauce
10 to 12 sandwich rolls, halved *or* 1 loaf artisan bread,
  sliced

SLOW COOKER DIRECTIONS

1. Combine beef, barbecue sauce and 1½ cups water in slow cooker. Cover; cook on LOW 2 hours.

2. To serve, shred with 2 forks and place on rolls.

Makes 10 to 12 sandwiches

Maple-Glazed Ham

4 slices ham (3 ounces each)
¼ cup maple syrup
1 teaspoon Dijon mustard

1. Preheat broiler.

2. Place ham slices on broiler pan. Combine syrup and mustard in small bowl. Brush each slice with about 1½ teaspoons of syrup mixture.

3. Broil 4 inches below heat about 4 minutes or until ham starts to brown. Turn and brush with remaining syrup mixture. Broil until browned. *Makes 4 servings*

BBQ Roast Beef

Ranch Chicken Tenders

2 tablespoons margarine or butter, melted
1 envelope LIPTON® RECIPE SECRETS® Ranch Soup Mix
1½ pounds chicken tenders or boneless, skinless chicken breast halves, cut in strips

1. In small bowl, combine margarine with soup mix. Add chicken to soup mixture and let stand 5 minutes.

2. Heat 10-inch nonstick skillet over medium-high heat 3 minutes or until hot.

3. Add chicken mixture and cook, stirring occasionally, 6 minutes or until chicken is thoroughly cooked. Serve, if desired, with your favorite dipping sauce, or on buns with lettuce, tomato, mayonnaise or mustard, or in warm flour tortillas with salsa. *Makes 4 servings*

Prep Time: 5 minutes
Cook Time: 6 minutes

E-Z Lemon 'n' Herb Roasted Chicken

1 whole (3½ to 4 pounds) fryer chicken
1 large SUNKIST® lemon, cut in half
   Fresh rosemary and/or thyme sprigs

For easy clean-up, line a 13×9×2-inch baking pan with aluminum foil. Spray a small roasting rack with nonstick cooking spray and place in baking pan. Remove neck and giblets from body cavity of chicken, and remove any excess fat; cut off tail. Rinse chicken well and pat dry with paper toweling. Place breast-side up on rack. Turn wing tips under back of chicken. With fingers, carefully separate skin from breast meat, starting at back and working towards neck end. Squeeze juice of ½ lemon; pour some under separated skin and remainder over top of breast, legs and wings. Cut remaining ½ lemon into 4 or 6 wedges and place in body cavity of chicken along with several herb sprigs. (It is not necessary to close body cavity with skewers or tie legs together.) Roast, uncovered, at 375°F. for 1¼ to 1½ hours until juices run clear when chicken is pierced in thickest part of thigh or internal temperature of thigh reaches 180°F., basting occasionally with pan drippings. Let stand 15 to 20 minutes before carving. To serve, arrange a few fresh herb sprigs at cavity opening. Garnish with lemon wedges, if desired.   *Makes 4 to 5 servings*

Sweet & Crispy Oven-Baked Chicken

1 pound boneless skinless chicken breast halves
¼ cup *French's®* Honey Mustard
1⅓ cups crushed *French's®* French Fried Onions

1. Coat chicken with mustard. Dip into French Fried Onions. Place into lightly greased baking pan.

2. Bake at 400°F for 20 minutes or until no longer pink in center.

Makes 4 servings

Prep Time: 5 minutes
Cook Time: 20 minutes

Grilled Veggie Burger

4 frozen veggie burgers
4 slices sweet onion, such as Vidalia
4 slices Swiss cheese

1. Preheat grill for direct cooking. Spray lightly with nonstick cooking spray.

2. Place burgers and onion slices on grill. Grill 5 minutes or until burgers are heated through and onion is soft, turning once.

3. Place cheese slices on burgers; top with onion slices. Serve immediately.

Makes 4 servings

Sweet & Crispy Oven-Baked Chicken

Glazed Pork Loin

1 bag (1 pound) baby carrots
4 boneless pork loin chops
1 jar (8 ounces) apricot preserves

SLOW COOKER DIRECTIONS

1. Place carrots on bottom of slow cooker. Place pork on carrots; brush with preserves.

2. Cover; cook on LOW 8 hours or on HIGH 4 hours.

Makes 4 servings

Grilled Fresh Fish

3 to 3½ pounds fresh tuna or catfish
¾ cup HIDDEN VALLEY® The Original Ranch® Salad Dressing
Chopped fresh dill
Lemon wedges (optional)

Place fish on heavy-duty foil. Cover with salad dressing. Grill over medium-hot coals until fish turns opaque and flakes easily when tested with fork, 20 to 30 minutes. Or, broil fish 15 to 20 minutes. Sprinkle with dill; garnish with lemon wedges, if desired.

Makes 6 servings

Glazed Pork Loin

String Cheese Spaghetti

1 box (16 ounces) spaghetti, cooked and drained
1 jar (1 pound 10 ounces) RAGÚ® Organic Pasta Sauce, heated
2 cups diced mozzarella cheese (about 8 ounces)

In large serving bowl, toss all ingredients. Garnish, if desired, with grated Parmesan cheese and chopped fresh parsley.

Makes 6 servings

Prep Time: 20 minutes

Lipton® Onion Burgers

1 envelope LIPTON® RECIPE SECRETS® Onion Soup Mix*
2 pounds ground beef
½ cup water

*Also terrific with LIPTON® RECIPE SECRETS® Beefy Onion, Onion Mushroom, Beefy Mushroom, Savory Herb with Garlic or Ranch Soup Mix.

1. In large bowl, combine all ingredients; shape into 8 patties.

2. Grill or broil until done.

Makes 8 servings

Prep Time: 10 minutes
Cook Time: 12 minutes

String Cheese Spaghetti

Louisiana Hot and Spicy Shrimp

1½ pounds uncooked medium shrimp, peeled and deveined
1 cup LAWRY'S® Louisiana Red Pepper Marinade With
 Lemon Juice
Wooden skewers, soaked in water for 15 minutes

In large resealable plastic bag, combine shrimp and ¾ cup Louisiana Red Pepper Marinade; turn to coat. Close bag and marinate in refrigerator for 30 minutes. Remove shrimp from Marinade, discard Marindade.

On wooden skewers, thread shrimp. Grill, brushing with remaining ¼ cup Marinade, until shrimp turn pink.   *Makes 6 servings*

Prep Time: 10 minutes
Marinate Time: 30 minutes
Cook Time: 6 minutes

Louisiana Hot and Spicy Shrimp

Magic Grilled Turkey Burgers

1 pound ground turkey
4 teaspoons water
4 teaspoons Chef Paul Prudhomme's Poultry Magic®,
   divided*

*Any of Chef Paul's Magic Seasoning Blends® will work well in this recipe. If you prefer a less seasoned dish, simply cut back the amount of Poultry Magic® that you use.

Combine meat, water and 2 teaspoons Poultry Magic® and fold in gently. Shape mixture into 4 patties, about 4 ounces each. Season patties evenly on both sides with remaining 2 teaspoons of Poultry Magic®. Place patties on grill and cook, turning several times, until patties are nicely browned on both sides and cooked through. (At least 160°F in center. Use meat thermometer to be sure they are fully cooked.)

Serve immediately with all your favorite hamburger fixings.

Makes 4 servings

Veggie Ravioli

2 cans (15 ounces each) ravioli
1 bag (16 ounces) BIRDS EYE® frozen Mixed Vegetables
2 cups shredded mozzarella cheese

• In 1½-quart microwave-safe casserole dish, combine ravioli and vegetables.

• Cover; microwave on HIGH 10 minutes, stirring halfway through cook time.

• Uncover; sprinkle with cheese. Microwave 5 minutes more or until cheese is melted.   *Makes 6 servings*

Serving Suggestion: Sprinkle with grated Parmesan cheese.

Prep Time: 5 minutes
Cook Time: 15 minutes

Smothered Mozzarella Sandwiches

4 hero rolls, halved lengthwise
1 package (8 ounces) mozzarella cheese, sliced
1 cup RAGÚ® Organic Pasta Sauce, heated

1. Preheat oven to 425°F. On baking sheet, arrange rolls. Place cheese on bottom halves of rolls.

2. Bake 10 minutes or until cheese is melted and rolls are lightly toasted. Evenly spoon Pasta Sauce over cheese. Serve, if desired, with additional heated Sauce for dipping. *Makes 4 servings*

Prep Time: 5 minutes
Cook Time: 10 minutes

Baked Salmon

1 (4 ounce) salmon fillet
1 teaspoon fresh lemon juice
½ teaspoon Cajun seasoning mix

1. Preheat oven to 325°F. Rinse salmon and pat dry. Place in center of large triangle of parchment paper on baking sheet. Sprinkle salmon with lemon juice and seasoning.

2. Double fold sides and ends of parchment paper to form package, leaving head space for heat circulation. Bake 20 to 25 minutes. Carefully open packet to allow steam to escape. Salmon is done when it flakes easily with fork. *Makes 1 serving*

Smothered Mozzarella Sandwich

Crispy Onion Crescent Rolls

1 can (8 ounces) refrigerated crescent dinner rolls
1⅓ cups *French's*® French Fried Onions, slightly crushed
1 egg, beaten

Preheat oven to 375°F. Line large baking sheet with foil. Separate refrigerated rolls into 8 triangles. Sprinkle center of each triangle with about 1½ tablespoons French Fried Onions. Roll up triangles from short side, jelly-roll fashion. Sprinkle any excess onions over top of crescents.

Arrange crescents on prepared baking sheet. Brush with beaten egg. Bake 15 minutes or until golden brown and crispy. Transfer to wire rack; cool slightly. *Makes 8 servings*

Prep Time: 15 minutes
Cook Time: 15 minutes

Herbed Corn on the Cob

1 tablespoon butter or margarine
1 teaspoon mixed dried herbs (such as basil, oregano, sage and rosemary)
4 ears corn, husks removed

MICROWAVE DIRECTIONS

1. Combine butter and herbs in small microwavable bowl. Microwave on MEDIUM (50%) 30 to 45 seconds or until butter is melted.

2. With pastry brush, coat corn with butter mixture. Place corn on microwavable plate; microwave on HIGH 5 to 6 minutes. Turn corn over; microwave on HIGH 5 to 6 minutes or until tender. Season with salt and black pepper, if desired.

Makes 4 servings

tip

When buying fresh corn, the husks should be green and the kernels should be plump and tightly packed. Keep cobs refrigerated.

Herbed Corn on the Cob

Sweet & Tangy Coleslaw

1 small bag (16 ounces) shredded cabbage
½ cup mayonnaise
½ cup *French's®* Honey Mustard

1. Combine ingredients in large bowl until blended.

2. Chill until ready to serve.   *Makes 6 to 8 servings*

Prep Time: 5 minutes

Pasta Primavera Salad

8 ounces uncooked rotini, cooked and drained
2½ cups blanched mixed vegetables
1 cup Italian salad dressing

Combine all ingredients in large bowl; mix well. Chill at least
30 minutes before serving.   *Makes 6 servings*

Low-Fat Cajun Wedges

4 medium russet potatoes
1 tablespoon Cajun seasoning or other seasoning, such as paprika
Purple kale and fresh sage leaves, for garnish

1. Preheat oven to 400°F. To prepare potatoes, scrub under running water with soft vegetable brush; rinse. Dry well. (Do not peel.) Line baking sheet with foil and spray with nonstick cooking spray.

2. Cut potatoes in half lengthwise; then cut each half lengthwise into 3 wedges. Place potatoes, skin side down, in single layer on prepared baking sheet. Spray potatoes lightly with additional cooking spray and sprinkle with seasoning.

3. Bake 25 minutes or until browned and fork-tender. Serve immediately. *Makes 4 servings*

Low-Fat Potato Chips: Follow step 1 as directed. Slice potatoes crosswise as thin as possible with chef's knife or mandoline slicer. Place in single layer on prepared baking sheet; spray and season as directed. Bake 10 to 15 minutes or until browned and crisp. Serve immediately.

Low-Fat Cottage Fries: Follow step 1 as directed. Cut potatoes crosswise into ¼-inch-thick slices. Place in single layer on prepared baking sheet; spray and season as directed. Bake 15 to 20 minutes or until browned and fork-tender. Serve immediately.

Grilled Coriander Corn

4 ears fresh corn
3 tablespoons butter or margarine, softened
1 teaspoon ground coriander

1. Pull outer husks from top to base of each corn; leave husks attached to ear. (If desired, remove 1 strip of husk from inner portion of each ear; reserve for later use.) Strip away silk from corn.

2. Place corn in large bowl. Cover with cold water; soak 20 to 30 minutes.

3. Meanwhile, prepare grill for direct cooking.

4. Remove corn from water; pat kernels dry with paper towels. Combine butter and coriander in small bowl. Spread evenly over kernels.

5. Bring husks back up each ear of corn; secure at top with paper-covered metal twist-ties. (Or, use reserved strips of corn husk to tie knots at the top of each ear, if desired.)

6. Place corn on grid. Grill corn, on covered grill, over medium-hot coals 20 to 25 minutes or until corn is hot and tender, turning halfway through grilling time. Season with salt and ground red pepper, if desired.   *Makes 4 servings*

Note: For ember cooking, prepare corn as recipe directs, but omit soaking in cold water. Wrap each ear securely in heavy-duty foil. Place directly on coals. Grill corn, in covered grill, on medium-hot coals 25 to 30 minutes or until corn is hot and tender, turning every 10 minutes with tongs.

Onion-Roasted Potatoes

1 envelope LIPTON® RECIPE SECRETS® Onion Soup Mix*
4 medium all-purpose potatoes, cut into large chunks (about 2 pounds)
⅓ cup BERTOLLI® Olive Oil

*Also terrific with LIPTON® RECIPE SECRETS® Onion Mushroom, Golden Onion or Savory Herb with Garlic Soup Mix.

1. Preheat oven to 450°F. In 13×9-inch baking or roasting pan, combine all ingredients.

2. Bake uncovered, stirring occasionally, 40 minutes or until potatoes are tender and golden brown.   *Makes 4 servings*

Prep Time: 10 minutes
Cook Time: 40 minutes

tip

Keep the skins on! Potato skins are a great source of iron, potassium and fiber.

Onion-Roasted Potatoes

Table of Contents

Starters & Snacks

Buffalo Rolls

¾ **pound JENNIE-O TURKEY STORE® Deli Premium Seasoned Buffalo Style Turkey Breast, thinly sliced**
½ **cup bleu cheese salad dressing, prepared**
5 **stalks celery, cut into sticks 3½×½×½ inches**
2 **ounces bleu cheese, crumbled**

Lay thin slice of JENNIE-O TURKEY STORE® Premium Seasoned Buffalo Style Seasoned Turkey Breast on flat surface. Spread turkey with thin layer of dressing. Place single celery stick on short edge of turkey slice and roll up tightly. Repeat with remaining turkey slices and ingredients. Lay rolls on appetizer platter, seam side down. Sprinkle lightly with crumbled bleu cheese. Serve.

Makes 18 to 25 pieces

Variations: Any variety of JENNIE-O TURKEY STORE® turkey breast can be used in this recipe. Add shredded carrot or green onion to the rolls. Experiment with your favorite bleu cheese types such as Stilton, Gorgonzola, etc.

Prep Time: 10 minutes

4 ingredient cookbook

Hot & Spicy Buffalo Chicken Wings

1 can (15 ounces) DEL MONTE® Original Sloppy Joe Sauce
¼ cup thick and chunky salsa, medium
1 tablespoon red wine vinegar or cider vinegar
20 chicken wings (about 4 pounds)

1. Preheat oven to 400°F.

2. Combine sloppy joe sauce, salsa and vinegar in small bowl. Remove ¼ cup sauce mixture to serve with cooked chicken wings; cover and refrigerate. Set aside remaining sauce mixture.

3. Arrange wings in single layer in large, shallow baking pan; brush wings with remaining sauce mixture.

4. Bake chicken, uncovered, on middle rack in oven 35 minutes or until chicken is no longer pink in center, turning and brushing with remaining sauce mixture after 15 minutes. Serve with reserved ¼ cup sauce. Garnish, if desired. *Makes 4 servings*

Prep Time: 5 minutes
Cook Time: 35 minutes

Hot & Spicy Buffalo Chicken Wings

Chili Kabobs

1 large poblano chile*
4 ounces smoked turkey breast, cut into 8 cubes
4 ounces pepper-jack cheese, chilled and cut into 8 cubes
¼ cup salsa

*Chiles can sting and irritate the skin, so wear rubber gloves when handling peppers and do not touch your eyes.

1. Preheat toaster oven to 400°F. Soak 4 wooden skewers in cold water 10 minutes. Drain and set aside. Place chile in pot of boiling water. Cook for 1 minute. Drain well. Core, seed and cut chile into 12 bite-size pieces.

2. Place 1 piece chile onto wooden skewer. Add 1 piece turkey; 1 piece cheese. Follow with 1 piece chile, 1 piece turkey and 1 piece cheese; end with chile. Repeat with remaining 3 skewers.

3. Place kabobs on toaster oven baking pan. Bake 3 minutes or until cheese starts to melt. Remove immediately. Serve with salsa on the side. *Makes 4 servings*

 Tip: If spicy foods aren't your thing, try these kabobs with chunks of sweet red bell pepper and cubes of Cheddar cheese.

Chili Kabobs

Starters & Snacks

Olive Twists

1 (11-ounce) package refrigerated breadsticks
1 egg white, beaten
Paprika
12 pimiento-stuffed olives, chopped

Preheat oven to 375°F degrees. Line a baking sheet with parchment paper. Separate breadsticks; brush dough lightly with egg white. Sprinkle with paprika and chopped green olives. Twist each stick 3 or 4 times. Bake 11 to 13 minutes or until golden. *Makes 12 servings*

Grilled Corn Soup

4 ears Grilled Corn-on-the-Cob (recipe follows)
5 green onions
4 cups chicken broth, divided
Salt and black pepper

Cut kernels from cobs to make 2 to 2½ cups. Slice green onions, separating the white part from the green. Place corn, white part of onions and 2 cups chicken broth in blender or food processor; process until mixture is slightly lumpy. Place corn mixture in large saucepan; add remaining chicken broth. Simmer gently 15 minutes. Stir in sliced green onion tops; season to taste with salt and pepper.

Makes 4 to 6 servings

Grilled Corn-on-the-Cob: Turn back corn husks; do not remove. Remove silks with stiff brush; rinse corn under cold running water. Smooth husks back into position. Grill ears, on a covered grill, over medium-hot KINGSFORD® briquets, about 25 minutes or until tender, turning corn often. Remove husks and serve.

Olive Twists

Starters & Snacks

Cheesy Chips

10 wonton wrappers
2 tablespoons powdered American cheese or grated
   Parmesan cheese
2 teaspoons olive oil
⅛ teaspoon garlic powder

1. Preheat oven to 375°F. Spray baking sheet with nonstick cooking spray.

2. Diagonally cut each wonton wrapper in half, forming two triangles. Place in single layer on prepared baking sheet.

3. Combine cheese, oil and garlic powder in small bowl. Sprinkle over wonton triangles. Bake 6 to 8 minutes or until golden brown. Remove from oven. Cool completely. *Makes 4 servings*

Quick Garlic-Onion Ring

¼ cup finely chopped green onions
1 tablespoon butter, melted
2 cloves garlic, minced
1 package (16 ounces) refrigerated buttermilk biscuits

1. Preheat oven to 400°F. Combine onions, butter and garlic in small bowl; set aside.

2. Separate dough into individual biscuits. Gently pull apart each biscuit to separate into two halves, making 20 pieces.

3. Brush one side of each piece with garlic-onion mixture. Arrange pieces, onion-side up and overlapping, in 9-inch circle on ungreased baking sheet. Bake 10 to 12 minutes until golden brown.

Makes 10 servings

Starters & Snacks

Creamy Hot Artichoke Dip

1 can (14 ounces) artichoke hearts, drained and chopped
1 cup HELLMANN'S® or BEST FOODS® Real Mayonnaise
1 cup grated Parmesan cheese (about 4 ounces)
1 clove garlic, finely chopped or ¼ teaspoon Lawry's® Garlic
    Powder With Parsley (optional)

1. Preheat oven to 350°F.

2. In 1-quart casserole, combine all ingredients. Bake uncovered 25 minutes or until heated through. Serve with your favorite dippers. *Makes 2½ cups dip*

For a Spinach & Artichoke Dip: Add 1 package (10 ounces) frozen chopped spinach, thawed and squeezed dry.

For a Seafood Artichoke Dip: Add 1 can (6 ounces) crabmeat, drained and flaked.

For an Italian Artichoke Dip: Add ½ cup shredded mozzarella cheese and ¼ cup drained and chopped sun-dried tomatoes.

For a Roasted Red Pepper Artichoke Dip: Add ½ cup shredded mozzarella cheese and ½ cup drained and chopped roasted red peppers.

For a Mexican Artichoke Dip: Omit Parmesan cheese and add 1 can (4 ounces) diced green chilies undrained, 1 cup shredded Monterey Jack cheese, ¼ cup chopped cilantro, ½ teaspoon ground cumin and hot pepper sauce to taste.

Prep Time: 5 minutes
Cook Time: 25 minutes

107

Starters & Snacks

Watermelon Kebobs

6 ounces (1-inch cubes) fat-free turkey breast
6 ounces (1-inch cubes) reduced-fat Cheddar cheese
18 cubes (1-inch) seedless watermelon
6 (6-inch) bamboo skewers

Alternate cubes of watermelon between cubes of turkey and cheese threaded onto each skewer, as shown in photo. *Makes 6 servings*

Favorite recipe from **National Watermelon Promotion Board**

Hidden Valley® Cheese Fingers

2 small loaves (8 ounces each) French bread, cut in half lengthwise
1 package (8 ounces) cream cheese, softened
1 packet (1 ounce) HIDDEN VALLEY® The Original Ranch® Salad Dressing & Seasoning Mix
4 cups assorted toppings, such as chopped onions, bell peppers and shredded cheese

Slice bread crosswise into 1-inch fingers, leaving fingers attached to crust. Mix together cream cheese and salad dressing & seasoning mix. Spread on cut sides of bread. Sprinkle on desired toppings. Broil about 3 minutes or until brown and bubbly.

Makes about 48 fingers

Watermelon Kebobs

Starters & Snacks

Bacon-Wrapped BBQ Chicken

8 chicken tender strips, patted dry (about 1 pound)
½ teaspoon paprika or cumin
8 slices bacon
½ cup barbecue sauce

1. Preheat broiler. Line broiler pan with foil and set aside.

2. Sprinkle chicken strips with paprika. Wrap each chicken strip with bacon in a spiral around the chicken and place on broiler pan.

3. Broil chicken 4 minutes; turn over and broil 2 minutes. Remove from oven and brush with ¼ cup barbecue sauce. Broil 2 minutes. Remove from oven, turn over chicken strips and baste with remaining barbecue sauce. Broil 2 minutes. Serve warm.

Makes 4 servings

Inside-Out Egg Salad

6 hard-cooked eggs, peeled
⅓ cup mayonnaise
¼ cup chopped celery
1 tablespoon *French's*® Classic Yellow® Mustard

1. Cut eggs in half lengthwise. Remove egg yolks. Combine yolks, mayonnaise, celery and mustard in small bowl. Add salt and pepper to taste.

2. Spoon egg yolk mixture into egg whites. Sprinkle with paprika, if desired. Chill before serving.

Makes 12 servings

Bacon-Wrapped BBQ Chicken

Starters & Snacks

Zucchini Pizza Bites

⅓ cup salsa

2 small zucchini, trimmed and cut diagonally into
¼-inch-thick slices

¼ pound chorizo sausage,* cooked, drained and crumbled

6 tablespoons shredded mozzarella cheese

Chorizo, a spicy pork sausage, is common in both Mexican and Spanish cooking. The Mexican variety (which is the kind most widely available in the U.S.) is made from raw pork while the Spanish variety is traditionally made from smoked pork. If chorizo is unavailable, substitute any variety of spicy sausage.

1. Preheat toaster oven to 400°F. Place salsa in fine sieve and press out excess moisture; set aside to drain.

2. Place zucchini on toaster oven tray. Spoon 1 teaspoon drained salsa on each zucchini slice. Top with chorizo, dividing evenly among zucchini slices. Sprinkle 1½ teaspoons cheese over each slice.

3. Bake 10 minutes or until cheese melts. Turn toaster oven to broil. Broil 30 seconds or until cheese is lightly browned. Remove from oven and serve.
Makes 6 servings

Tip: At the end of the summer, this recipe is a great way to use zucchini from your garden. Play with a variety of toppings to suit your tastes.

Zucchini Pizza Bites

Starters & Snacks

Super Nachos

12 large tortilla chips
½ cup (2 ounces) shredded Cheddar cheese
¼ cup refried beans
2 tablespoons chunky salsa

MICROWAVE DIRECTIONS

1. Arrange chips in single layer on large microwavable plate. Sprinkle cheese evenly over chips.

2. Spoon 1 teaspoon beans over each chip; top with ½ teaspoon salsa.

3. Microwave on MEDIUM (50%) 1½ minutes; rotate dish. Microwave 1 to 1½ minutes more or until cheese is melted.

Makes 2 servings

Conventional Directions: Preheat oven to 350°F. Substitute foil-covered baking sheet for microwavable plate. Assemble nachos on prepared baking sheet as directed above. Bake 10 to 12 minutes or until cheese is melted.

Tip: For a single serving of nachos, arrange 6 large tortilla chips on microwavable plate; top each chip with 2 teaspoons cheese, 1 teaspoon refried beans and ½ teaspoon salsa. Microwave on MEDIUM (50%) 1 minute; rotate dish. Microwave 30 seconds to 1 minute or until cheese is melted.

Super Nachos

Starters & Snacks

Turkey & Havarti Roll-ups

2 slices turkey
2 slices Havarti cheese
2 tablespoons Dijon-style mayonnaise
4 thin slices apple

Place Havarti on turkey and spread with mayonnaise. Top with apple slices and roll. *Makes 2 roll-ups*

Pepperoni Pizza Dip

1 cup RAGÚ® Old World Style® Pasta Sauce
1 cup RAGÚ® Cheesy! Classic Alfredo Sauce
1 cup shredded mozzarella cheese (about 4 ounces)
¼ to ½ cup finely chopped pepperoni

1. In 2-quart saucepan, heat Ragú Pasta Sauces, cheese and pepperoni, stirring occasionally, 10 minutes or until cheese is melted.

2. Pour into 1½-quart casserole or serving dish and serve, if desired, with breadsticks, sliced Italian bread or crackers. *Makes 2 cups dip*

Prep Time: 5 minutes
Cook Time: 10 minutes

Turkey & Havarti Roll-ups

Starters & Snacks

Ham, Apple and Cheese Turnovers

1¼ cups chopped cooked ham
¾ cup finely chopped red apple
¾ cup (3 ounces) shredded Cheddar cheese
1 tablespoon brown mustard (optional)
1 package (about 14 ounces) refrigerated pizza dough

1. Preheat oven to 400°F. Spray large baking sheet with nonstick cooking spray. Combine ham, apple, cheese and mustard, if desired, in medium bowl; set aside.

2. Roll pizza dough into 15×10-inch rectangle on a lightly floured surface. Cut into six (5-inch) squares. Top each square with ⅙ of ham mixture. Moisten edges with water. Fold dough over filling. Press edges to seal. Place on prepared baking sheet.

3. Prick tops of each turnover with fork. Bake about 15 minutes or until golden brown. Serve warm. Refrigerate leftovers.

Makes 6 servings

Prep Time: 15 minutes
Bake Time: 15 minutes

Ham, Apple and Cheese Turnovers

Pizza & Pasta

Chicken Parmesan Pasta Toss

1 jar (1 pound 10 ounces) RAGÚ® Organic Pasta Sauce
**8 ounces fusilli, bucati or your favorite pasta, cooked and
    drained**
**1 package (12 ounces) baked breaded low-fat chicken
    breast tenders, heated according to package directions**
2 cups shredded mozzarella cheese (about 8 ounces)

In 2-quart saucepan, heat Pasta Sauce.

In large serving bowl, combine heated Sauce, pasta, chicken and
1 cup cheese. Top with remaining 1 cup cheese and serve
immediately.   *Makes 4 servings*

Prep Time: 20 minutes

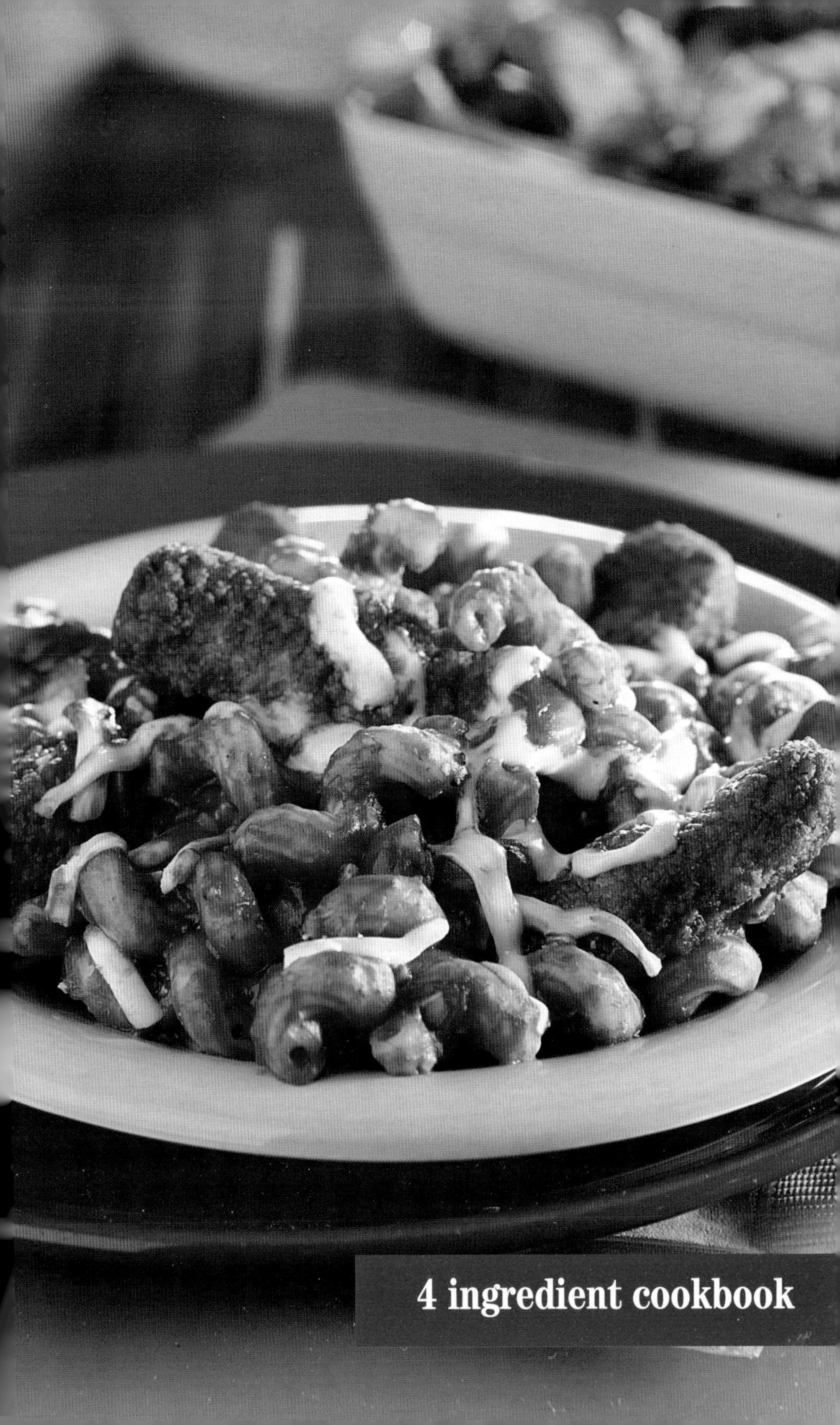
4 ingredient cookbook

Pizza & Pasta

Pepperoni Pasta Salad

1 bag (16 ounces) BIRDS EYE® frozen Broccoli, Red Peppers, Onions and Mushrooms
2 cups cooked macaroni
1 package (3 ounces) thinly sliced pepperoni
¼ to ½ cup peppercorn or ranch salad dressing

• Cook vegetables according to package directions; drain.

• Combine vegetables and macaroni in large bowl. Chill.

• Toss with pepperoni and dressing. Add salt and pepper to taste.

Makes 4 to 6 servings

Prep Time: 2 minutes, plus chilling time
Cook Time: 10 to 12 minutes

BelGioioso® Fontina Melt

1 loaf Italian or French bread
2 fresh tomatoes, cubed
Basil leaves, julienned
BELGIOIOSO® Fontina Cheese, sliced

Cut bread lengthwise into halves. Top each half with tomatoes and sprinkle with basil. Top with BelGioioso Fontina Cheese. Place in oven at 350°F for 10 to 12 minutes or until cheese is golden brown.

Makes 6 to 8 servings

Pepperoni Pasta Salad

Pizza & Pasta

Upside-Down Deep Dish Pizza

1 jar (2 pounds) RAGÚ® Rich & Meaty Meat Sauce
1 package (10 ounces) frozen chopped spinach or broccoli, thawed and squeezed dry (optional)
2 cups shredded mozzarella cheese (about 8 ounces)
1 can (10 ounces) refrigerated pizza dough

Preheat oven to 375°. In 2-quart baking dish, pour Meat Sauce. Evenly top with spinach, then cheese. Place pizza crust over dish, sealing edges tightly. Bake 20 minutes or until lightly browned. Let stand 10 minutes
Makes 4 servings

Cook Time: 20 minutes
Prep Time: 5 minutes

Baked Manicotti

1 jar (1 pound 10 ounces) RAGÚ® Old World Style® Pasta Sauce
8 fresh or frozen prepared manicotti
½ cup (about 2 ounces) shredded mozzarella cheese
2 tablespoons grated Parmesan cheese

Preheat oven to 450°F. In 13×9-inch baking dish, spread ½ of the Ragú Old World Style Pasta Sauce; arrange manicotti over sauce. Top with remaining sauce. Sprinkle with cheeses. Bake covered 20 minutes. Remove cover and continue baking 5 minutes or until heated through.
Makes 4 servings

Upside-Down Deep Dish Pizza

Pizza & Pasta

Skillet Shrimp Scampi

2 teaspoons BERTOLLI® Olive Oil
2 pounds uncooked shrimp, peeled and deveined
⅔ cup LAWRY'S® Herb & Garlic Marinade
¼ cup finely chopped green onion, including tops

In large nonstick skillet, heat oil over medium heat. Add shrimp and Herb & Garlic Marinade. Cook, stirring often, until shrimp turn pink, about 3 to 5 minutes. Stir in green onions.

Makes 4 to 6 servings

Meal Idea: Serve over hot, cooked rice, orzo or your favorite pasta.

Variations: This dish is wonderful served chilled with toothpicks as an appetizer. Try serving chilled then tossed in a pasta or green salad. Take it to your next picnic! Also delicious using LAWRY'S® Lemon Pepper Marinade.

Prep Time: 5 minutes
Cook Time: 3 to 5 minutes

Skillet Shrimp Scampi

Pizza & Pasta

Pizza Pinwheels

2 packages (13.8 ounces each) refrigerated pizza crust dough
1 jar (1 pound 10 ounces) RAGÚ® ROBUSTO!® Pasta Sauce
1 cup shredded mozzarella cheese (about 4 ounces)
1 cup sliced pepperoni, chopped (about 4 ounces)

Preheat oven to 425°F. With rolling pin or hands, press each pizza crust dough into 8×12-inch rectangle, then cut each into 4 equal squares.

On two greased baking sheets, arrange squares. With knife, starting at corner of each square, cut toward center of square stopping ½-inch from center. Evenly top each square with 2 tablespoons Pasta Sauce, then cheese and pepperoni. Fold every other point into center; press to seal. Bake 10 minutes or until crusts are golden. Serve with remaining Sauce, heated.   *Makes 8 pinwheels*

Prep Time: 15 minutes
Cook Time: 10 minutes

Tip: Make these pinwheels meatless by skipping the pepperoni and substituting chopped sauteed mushrooms and spinach.

Pizza Pinwheel

Pizza & Pasta

Vegetable Pizza

2 to 3 cups BIRDS EYE® frozen Broccoli, Red Peppers, Onions and Mushrooms
1 Italian bread shell or pizza crust, about 12 inches
1 to 1½ cups shredded mozzarella cheese
Dried oregano, basil or Italian seasoning

• Preheat oven according to directions on pizza crust package.

• Rinse vegetables in colander under warm water. Drain well; pat with paper towel to remove excess moisture.

• Spread crust with half the cheese and all the vegetables. Sprinkle with herbs; top with remaining cheese.

• Follow baking directions on pizza crust package; bake until hot and bubbly. *Makes 3 to 4 servings*

Prep Time: 5 minutes
Cook Time: 15 minutes

Vegetable Pizza

Pizza & Pasta

Olive Lover's Pasta

1 jar (1 pound 10 ounces) RAGÚ® ROBUSTO!® Pasta Sauce
1 package (12 ounces) tri-color pasta twists, cooked and drained
1 cup sliced assorted pitted olives
2 tablespoons grated Parmesan cheese

In 2-quart saucepan, heat Pasta Sauce over medium-low heat. To serve, toss hot pasta with Sauce and olives, then sprinkle with cheese. *Makes 6 servings*

Prep Time: 20 minutes
Cook Time: 5 minutes

Mac and Cheese Toss

8 ounces oven-baked deli ham, diced
4 cups prepared deli macaroni and cheese (1 quart)
½ cup frozen green peas, thawed
¼ cup milk or cream

1. Combine all ingredients in microwavable 2-quart casserole. Toss gently until combined. Cover with plastic wrap.

2. Microwave on HIGH 3 minutes; stir. Microwave 1 minute more or until heated through. *Makes 4 servings*

Note: To thaw peas quickly, place peas in a small colander and run under cold water 15 to 20 seconds or until thawed. Shake off liquid.

Olive Lover's Pasta

Pizza & Pasta

Pasta Fagioli

**1 jar (1 pound 10 ounces) RAGÚ® Chunky Gardenstyle
  Pasta Sauce
1 can (19 ounces) white kidney beans, rinsed and drained
1 box (10 ounces) frozen chopped spinach, thawed
8 ounces ditalini pasta, cooked and drained (reserve 2 cups
  pasta water)**

1. In 6-quart saucepot, combine Ragú Pasta Sauce, beans, spinach, pasta and reserved pasta water; heat through.

2. Season, if desired, with salt, ground black pepper and grated Parmesan cheese. *Makes 4 servings*

Prep Time: 20 minutes
Cook Time: 10 minutes

Tip: Serve this hearty soup with slices of crusty Italian bread and olive oil and Parmesan cheese for dipping.

Pasta Fagioli

Dinner-Time Delights

Grilled Garlic-Pepper Shrimp

⅓ cup olive oil
2 tablespoons lemon juice
1 teaspoon garlic pepper blend
20 jumbo shrimp, peeled and deveined

1. Combine oil, lemon juice and garlic pepper in large resealable food storage bag; add shrimp. Marinate 20 to 30 minutes in refrigerator, turning bag once.

2. Meanwhile, spray grid with nonstick cooking spray. Prepare grill for direct cooking.

3. Thread 5 shrimp onto each of 4 skewers;* discard marinade. Grill on grid over medium heat 6 minutes or until pink and opaque. Serve with lemon wedges, if desired. *Makes 4 servings*

If using wooden skewers, soak in water 20 minutes before using to prevent burning.

4 ingredient cookbook

Dinner-Time Delights

Easy Veggie-Topped Spuds

2½ cups frozen broccoli-carrot vegetable medley
4 large baking potatoes
1 can (10¾ ounces) condensed cream of broccoli and cheese soup, undiluted
½ cup (2 ounces) shredded Cheddar cheese

MICROWAVE DIRECTIONS

1. Place vegetables in microwavable bowl. Microwave on HIGH 5 minutes; drain.

2. Scrub potatoes; pierce several times with knife. Microwave on HIGH 15 minutes or until potatoes are soft.

3. While potatoes are cooking, combine soup, vegetables and cheese in medium saucepan. Cook and stir over low heat until cheese melts and mixture is heated through.

4. Split potatoes lengthwise in half. Top each potato with soup mixture. Season to taste with salt and black pepper.

Makes 4 servings

Tip: Store potatoes in a cool, dark place away from onions for up to 2 weeks. (Storing potatoes and onions together will cause the potatoes to rot more quickly.)

Prep and Cook Time: 23 minutes

Easy Veggie-Topped Spuds

Dinner-Time Delights

Beef Caesar Salad

1 boneless beef top sirloin steak (about 1 pound)
1 bag (10 ounces) ready-to-use chopped romaine lettuce
2 tablespoons Caesar salad dressing
2 slices whole wheat bread, toasted and cut into 32 croutons

1. Cut steak lengthwise in half, then crosswise into ⅛-inch-thick strips. Spray 12-inch nonstick skillet with nonstick cooking spray and heat over high heat. Add beef; stir-fry 2 minutes or until beef is tender.

2. Toss lettuce and dressing in large bowl. Divide salad greens evenly among 4 plates.

3. Top each plate of lettuce mixture with ¼ of steak strips. Season with black pepper, if desired, and top with croutons.

Makes 4 servings

Sweet 'n' Spicy Chicken

1 bottle (8 ounces) WISH-BONE® Russian Dressing
1 envelope LIPTON® RECIPE SECRETS® Onion Soup Mix
1 jar (12 ounces) apricot preserves
2½ to 3-pound chicken, cut into serving pieces

1. Preheat oven to 425°F. In small bowl, combine Wish-Bone Russian Dressing, soup mix and preserves.

2. In 13×9-inch baking dish, arrange chicken; pour on dressing mixture. Bake uncovered, basting occasionally with dressing mixture, 40 minutes or until chicken is thoroughly cooked. Serve, if desired, with hot cooked rice.

Makes 6 servings

Beef Caesar Salad

Dinner-Time Delights

Wasabi Salmon

2 tablespoons soy sauce
1½ teaspoons wasabi paste or wasabi prepared from powder, divided, plus more to taste
4 salmon fillets (6 ounces each), with skin
¼ cup mayonnaise

1. Prepare grill or preheat broiler. Combine soy sauce and ½ teaspoon wasabi paste; mix well. Spoon mixture over salmon. Place salmon, skin sides down, on grid over medium coals or on rack of broiler pan. Grill or broil 4 to 5 inches from heat source 8 minutes or until salmon is opaque in center.

2. Meanwhile, combine mayonnaise and remaining 1 teaspoon wasabi paste; mix well. Taste and add more wasabi, if desired. Transfer salmon to serving plates; top with mayonnaise mixture.

Makes 4 servings

Tip: Wasabi is sometimes referred to as Japanese horseradish. It has an intense fiery flavor that doesn't linger in your mouth. Go easy on the wasabi if trying for the first time!

Wasabi Salmon

Dinner-Time Delights

Onion-Baked Pork Chops

1 envelope LIPTON® RECIPE SECRETS® Golden Onion Soup Mix*
⅓ cup plain dry bread crumbs
4 pork chops, 1 inch thick (about 3 pounds)
1 egg, well beaten

*Also terrific with LIPTON® RECIPE SECRETS® Onion or Savory Herb with Garlic Soup Mix.

1. Preheat oven to 400°F. In small bowl, combine soup mix and bread crumbs. Dip chops in egg, then bread crumb mixture until evenly coated.

2. On baking sheet arrange chops.

3. Bake uncovered 20 minutes or until done, turning once.

Makes 4 servings

Oriental Beef Kabobs

1 tablespoon olive oil
1 tablespoon seasoned rice vinegar
1 tablespoon soy sauce
4 purchased beef kabobs

1. Preheat broiler.

2. Whisk together oil, vinegar and soy sauce; brush on kabobs.

3. Arrange kabobs on broiler rack. Broil, 4 inches from heat source, 10 minutes or to desired doneness, turning after 5 minutes.

Makes 4 servings

Onion-Baked Pork Chop

Dinner-Time Delights

Marinated Flank Steak with Pineapple

**1 can (15¼ ounces) DEL MONTE® Sliced Pineapple In Its
   Own Juice**
¼ cup teriyaki sauce
2 tablespoons honey
1 pound beef flank steak

1. Drain pineapple, reserving 2 tablespoons juice. Set aside pineapple for later use.

2. Combine reserved juice, teriyaki sauce and honey in shallow 2-quart dish; mix well. Add meat; turn to coat. Cover and refrigerate at least 30 minutes or overnight.

3. Remove meat from marinade, reserving marinade. Grill meat over hot coals (or broil), brushing occasionally with reserved marinade. Cook about 4 minutes on each side for rare; about 5 minutes on each side for medium; or about 6 minutes on each side for well done. During last 4 minutes of cooking, grill pineapple until heated through.

4. Slice meat across grain; serve with pineapple. Garnish, if desired.

Makes 4 servings

Note: Marinade that has come into contact with raw meat must be discarded or boiled for several minutes before serving with cooked food.

Prep and Marinate Time: 35 minutes
Cook Time: 10 minutes

146

Dinner-Time Delights

Sweet & Zesty Fish with Fruit Salsa

¼ cup *French's*® Spicy Brown Mustard
¼ cup honey
2 cups chopped assorted fresh fruit (pineapple, kiwi, strawberries and mango)
1 pound sea bass or cod fillets or other firm-fleshed white fish

1. Preheat broiler or grill. Combine mustard and honey. Stir *2 tablespoons* mustard mixture into fruit; set aside.

2. Brush remaining mustard mixture on both sides of fillets. Place in foil-lined broiler pan. Broil (or grill) fish 6 inches from heat for 8 minutes or until fish is opaque.

3. Serve fruit salsa with fish.   *Makes 4 servings*

Tip: To prepare this meal even faster, purchase cut-up fresh fruit from the salad bar.

Prep Time: 15 minutes
Cook Time: 8 minutes

Dinner-Time Delights

Shrimp Robusto

2 tablespoons olive oil
¼ teaspoon crushed red pepper flakes
1 pound uncooked shrimp, peeled and deveined
1 jar (1 pound 10 ounces) RAGÚ® ROBUSTO!® Pasta Sauce

In 12-inch skillet, heat olive oil over medium-high heat and cook red pepper flakes, stirring occasionally, 1 minute. Add shrimp and cook 3 minutes. Stir in Pasta Sauce. Simmer 5 minutes or until shrimp is done and Sauce is heated through.   *Makes 4 servings*

Prep Time: 10 minutes
Cook Time: 10 minutes

Citrus Glazed Ham Steak

2 fully cooked ham steaks, cut ½ inch thick (about 2 pounds)
⅓ cup *French's®* Spicy Brown Mustard
¼ cup honey or molasses
½ teaspoon grated orange peel

Remove fat from edges of ham steaks with sharp knife. Combine mustard, honey and orange peel in small bowl. Brush on ham. Place ham on grid. Grill over medium-hot coals until steaks are glazed and heated through, basting often with mustard mixture. Serve warm.   *Makes 4 servings*

Prep Time: 5 minutes
Cook Time: 10 minutes

Shrimp Robusto

Dinner-Time Delights

Roast Garlic Chicken

1 whole broiler-fryer chicken (about 3 to 4 pounds)
2 tablespoons lemon juice
1½ teaspoons LAWRY'S® Garlic Powder With Parsley
2 teaspoons LAWRY'S® Seasoned Salt

Sprinkle chicken with lemon juice, Garlic Powder With Parsley and Seasoned Salt over outside and inside cavity of chicken. Spray 13×9×2-inch baking dish and roasting rack with nonstick cooking spray. Place chicken, breast side up, on roasting rack. Roast in 400°F oven 70 minutes, or until chicken is thoroughly cooked. Let stand 10 minutes before carving. *Makes 6 servings*

Hint: Loosely 'crunch up' some foil in the dish around the chicken to keep grease from splattering in the oven.

Prep Time: 10 minutes
Cook Time: 70 minutes

Roast Garlic Chicken

Dinner-Time Delights

Seafood Risotto

1 package (5.2 ounces) rice in creamy sauce (Risotto Milanese flavor)
1 package (14 to 16 ounces) frozen fully cooked shrimp
1 box (10 ounces) BIRDS EYE® frozen Mixed Vegetables
2 teaspoons grated Parmesan cheese

• In 4-quart saucepan, prepare rice according to package directions. Add frozen shrimp and vegetables during last 10 minutes of cooking.

• Sprinkle with cheese. *Makes 4 servings*

Prep Time: 5 minutes
Cook Time: 15 minutes

 Serve with garlic bread and a tossed green salad for a complete meal.

152

Seafood Risotto

Dinner-Time Delights

Rosemary-Crusted Leg of Lamb

¼ cup Dijon mustard
2 large cloves garlic, minced
1 boneless butterflied leg of lamb (sirloin half, about 2½ pounds), well trimmed
3 tablespoons chopped fresh rosemary *or* 1 tablespoon dried rosemary

1. Prepare grill for direct cooking.

2. Combine mustard and garlic in small bowl; spread half of mixture over one side of lamb. Sprinkle with half of chopped rosemary; pat into mustard mixture. Turn lamb over; repeat with remaining mustard mixture and rosemary. Insert meat thermometer into center of thickest part of lamb.

3. Place lamb on grid. Grill, covered, over medium coals 35 to 40 minutes or until thermometer registers 160°F for medium or until desired doneness is reached, turning every 10 minutes.

4. Transfer lamb to carving board; tent with foil. Let stand 10 minutes before carving into thin slices. Serve with mint jelly, if desired.
Makes 8 servings

Rosemary-Crusted Leg of Lamb

Dinner-Time Delights

Mustard-Grilled Red Snapper

½ cup Dijon mustard
1 tablespoon red wine vinegar
1 teaspoon ground red pepper
4 red snapper fillets (about 6 ounces each)

1. Spray grid with nonstick cooking spray. Prepare grill for direct cooking.

2. Combine mustard, vinegar and pepper in small bowl; mix well. Coat fish thoroughly with mustard mixture.

3. Place fish on grid. Grill, covered, over medium-high heat 8 minutes or until fish flakes easily when tested with fork, turning once halfway through grilling time. Garnish with parsley sprigs and red peppercorns, if desired. *Makes 4 servings*

Easy Beef Stroganoff

3 cans (10¾ ounces each) condensed cream of chicken or
**   cream of mushroom soup, undiluted**
1 cup sour cream
1 package (1 ounce) dry onion soup mix
2 pounds beef stew meat

SLOW COOKER DIRECTIONS

Combine soup, sour cream, ½ cup water and onion soup mix in slow cooker. Add beef; stir until well coated. Cover; cook on on LOW 6 hours or on HIGH 3 hours. *Makes 4 to 6 servings*

Serving Suggestion: Serve this beef over hot cooked wild rice or noodles along with a salad and grilled bread.

Mustard-Grilled Red Snapper

Cookie Jar Favorites

Mint Chip Thumbprints

2 packages (18 ounces each) refrigerated mini chocolate chip cookie dough
⅓ cup all-purpose flour
½ teaspoon peppermint extract
1 box (5 ounces) miniature (¾-inch) chocolate-covered mint candies

1. Let both packages of dough stand at room temperature about 15 minutes. Preheat oven to 350°F. Lightly grease cookie sheets.

2. Combine both doughs, flour and peppermint extract in large bowl; beat until well blended. Shape dough into 1-inch balls; place 2 inches apart on prepared cookie sheets.

3. Bake 5 minutes. Gently press one candy into each dough ball. Bake additional 4 to 6 minutes or until edges are light brown. Cool 2 minutes on cookie sheets. Remove to wire racks; cool completely.

Makes about 3½ dozen cookies

4 ingredient cookbook

Cookie Jar Favorites

Toffee Creme Sandwich Cookies

1 jar (7 ounces) marshmallow creme
¼ cup toffee baking bits
48 (2-inch) sugar or fudge-striped shortbread cookies
   Red and green sprinkles

1. Combine marshmallow creme and toffee bits in medium bowl until well blended. (Mixture will be stiff.)

2. Spread 1 teaspoon marshmallow mixture on bottom of 1 cookie; top with another cookie. Roll side of sandwich cookie in sprinkles. Repeat with remaining marshmallow creme mixture, cookies and sprinkles. *Makes 2 dozen cookies*

Prep Time: 20 minutes

Chocolate-Pecan Angels

1 cup mini semisweet chocolate chips
1 cup chopped pecans, toasted
1 cup sifted powdered sugar
1 egg white

1. Preheat oven to 350°F. Grease cookie sheets. Combine chocolate chips, pecans and powdered sugar in medium bowl. Add egg white; mix well. Drop by teaspoonfuls 2 inches apart onto prepared cookie sheets.

2. Bake 11 to 12 minutes or until edges are light golden brown. Let cookies stand on cookie sheets 1 minute. Remove cookies to wire racks; cool completely. *Makes about 3 dozen cookies*

Toffee Creme Sandwich Cookies

Cookie Jar Favorites

Flourless Peanut Butter Cookies

1 cup peanut butter
1 cup packed light brown sugar
1 egg
24 milk chocolate candy stars or milk chocolate candy kisses

1. Preheat oven to 350°F. Combine peanut butter, sugar and egg in medium bowl; beat until blended and smooth.

2. Shape dough into 24 balls. Place 2 inches apart on ungreased cookie sheets. Press one chocolate star on top of each cookie. Bake 10 to 12 minutes or until set. Transfer to wire racks to cool completely.

Makes 2 dozen cookies

Tip: Make these decadent cookies for a bake sale and they will be the first to go. Just don't tell anyone how simple they were to make!

Flourless Peanut Butter Cookies

Cookie Jar Favorites

Chocolate Toffee Crescents

1 package (18 ounces) refrigerated triple chocolate cookie dough
½ cup all-purpose flour
1 package (8 ounces) toffee baking bits
¾ cup butterscotch chips or semisweet chocolate chips

1. Let dough stand at room temperature about 15 minutes. Lightly grease cookie sheets.

2. Combine dough and flour in large bowl; beat until well blended. Stir in 1 cup toffee bits. Shape dough by rounded tablespoonfuls into crescent shapes; place 2 inches apart on prepared cookie sheets. Freeze 20 minutes.

3. Preheat oven to 350°F. Bake crescents 9 to 11 minutes or until set. Cool on cookie sheets 2 minutes. Remove to wire racks; cool completely.

4. Place butterscotch chips in small resealable food storage bag. Microwave on MEDIUM (50%) 1 minute; knead bag lightly. Microwave and knead at additional 30-second intervals until completely melted. Cut off tiny corner of bag. Drizzle melted chips over crescents; sprinkle with remaining toffee bits. Let stand until set. *Makes about 2 dozen cookies*

Chocolate Toffee Crescents

Cookie Jar Favorites

Nutty Lemon Crescents

1 package (18 ounces) refrigerated sugar cookie dough
1 cup chopped pecans, toasted*
1 tablespoon grated lemon peel
1½ cups powdered sugar, divided

*To toast pecans, spread in single layer on baking sheet. Bake in preheated 350°F oven 8 to 10 minutes or until golden brown, stirring frequently.

1. Let dough stand at room temperature about 15 minutes. Preheat oven to 375°F.

2. Combine dough, pecans and lemon peel in large bowl. Stir until thoroughly blended. Shape level tablespoonfuls of dough into crescent shapes. Place 2 inches apart on ungreased cookie sheets. Bake 8 to 9 minutes or until set and very lightly browned. Cool 2 minutes on cookie sheets. Remove to wire racks to cool completely.

3. Place 1 cup powdered sugar in shallow bowl. Roll warm cookies in powdered sugar. Cool completely. Sift remaining ½ cup powdered sugar over cookies just before serving.   *Makes about 4 dozen cookies*

Cookie Jar
Favorites

Elephant Ears

**1 package (17¼ ounces) frozen puff pastry, thawed according
to package directions**
1 egg, beaten
¼ cup sugar, divided
2 squares (1 ounce each) semisweet chocolate

1. Preheat oven to 375°F. Grease cookie sheets; sprinkle lightly with
water. Roll one sheet of pastry to 12×10-inch rectangle. Brush with
egg; sprinkle with 1 tablespoon sugar. Tightly roll up both 10-inch
sides, meeting in center. Brush center with egg and seal rolls tightly
together; turn over. Cut into ⅜-inch-thick slices. Place slices on
prepared cookie sheets. Sprinkle with 1 tablespoon sugar. Repeat
with remaining pastry, egg and sugar.

2. Bake 16 to 18 minutes until golden brown. Remove to wire racks;
cool completely.

3. Melt chocolate in small saucepan over low heat, stirring
constantly. Remove from heat. Spread bottoms of cookies with
chocolate. Place on wire rack, chocolate side up. Let stand until
chocolate is set. Store between layers of waxed paper in airtight
containers.   *Makes about 4 dozen cookies*

Cookie Jar Favorites

Apple Cinnamon Chunkies

**1 package (18 ounces) refrigerated oatmeal raisin
  cookie dough**
1 cup chopped dried apples
½ cup cinnamon baking chips
½ teaspoon apple pie spice*

**Substitute ¼ teaspoon ground cinnamon, ⅛ teaspoon ground nutmeg and
pinch of ground allspice or ground cloves for ½ teaspoon apple pie spice.*

1. Let dough stand at room temperature about 15 minutes. Preheat oven to 350°F. Lightly grease cookie sheets.

2. Combine dough, apples, cinnamon chips and apple pie spice in large bowl; beat until well blended. Drop dough by rounded tablespoonfuls 2 inches apart onto prepared cookie sheets.

3. Bake 10 to 12 minutes or until golden brown. Cool on cookie sheets 2 to 3 minutes. Remove to wire racks; cool completely.

Makes 2 dozen cookies

Apple Cinnamon Chunkies

Cookie Jar Favorites

Chocolate Chip Macaroons

2½ cups flaked coconut
⅔ cup mini semisweet chocolate chips
⅔ cup sweetened condensed milk
1 teaspoon vanilla

1. Preheat oven to 350°F. Grease cookie sheets. Combine coconut, chocolate chips, milk and vanilla in medium bowl; mix until well blended.

2. Drop dough by rounded teaspoonfuls 2 inches apart onto prepared cookie sheets. Press dough gently with back of spoon to flatten slightly. Bake 10 to 12 minutes or until light golden brown. Let cookies stand on cookie sheets 1 minute. Remove cookies to wire racks; cool completely. *Makes about 3½ dozen cookies*

Tip: Substitute chopped dried fruit or nuts for the chocolate chips in this recipe. The possibilities are endless.

Chocolate Chip Macaroons

Cookie Jar Favorites

Nutty Tropical Cookies

1 package (18 ounces) refrigerated chocolate chip and caramel cookie dough
2 cups flaked coconut
1½ cups macadamia nuts, chopped
1 to 1½ tablespoons grated orange peel

1. Let dough stand at room temperature about 15 minutes. Preheat oven to 350°F. Lightly grease cookie sheets.

2. Combine dough, coconut, nuts and orange peel in large bowl; beat until well blended. Shape dough into 1¼-inch balls; place 2 inches apart on prepared cookie sheets.

3. Bake about 15 minutes or until edges are brown and centers are set. Cool 2 minutes on cookie sheets. Remove to wire racks; cool completely.
Makes 2½ dozen cookies

172

Nutty Tropical Cookies

Indulgent Desserts

Candy Cups

> 1 package (18 ounces) refrigerated sugar cookie dough
> ⅓ cup all-purpose flour
> 1 package (12 ounces) bite-sized chocolate-covered peanut, caramel and nougat candy
> ¼ cup cocktail peanuts, chopped

1. Let dough stand at room temperature about 15 minutes. Preheat oven to 350°F. Lightly grease 36 mini (1¾-inch) muffin pan cups.

2. Combine dough and flour in large bowl; beat until well blended. Shape dough into 36 balls; press onto bottoms and up sides of prepared muffin cups. Place 1 candy into center of each muffin cup.

3. Bake 10 to 11 minutes or until edges are golden brown. Immediately sprinkle with peanuts. Cool 10 minutes in pan on wire racks. Remove to wire racks; cool completely.

Makes 3 dozen cookies

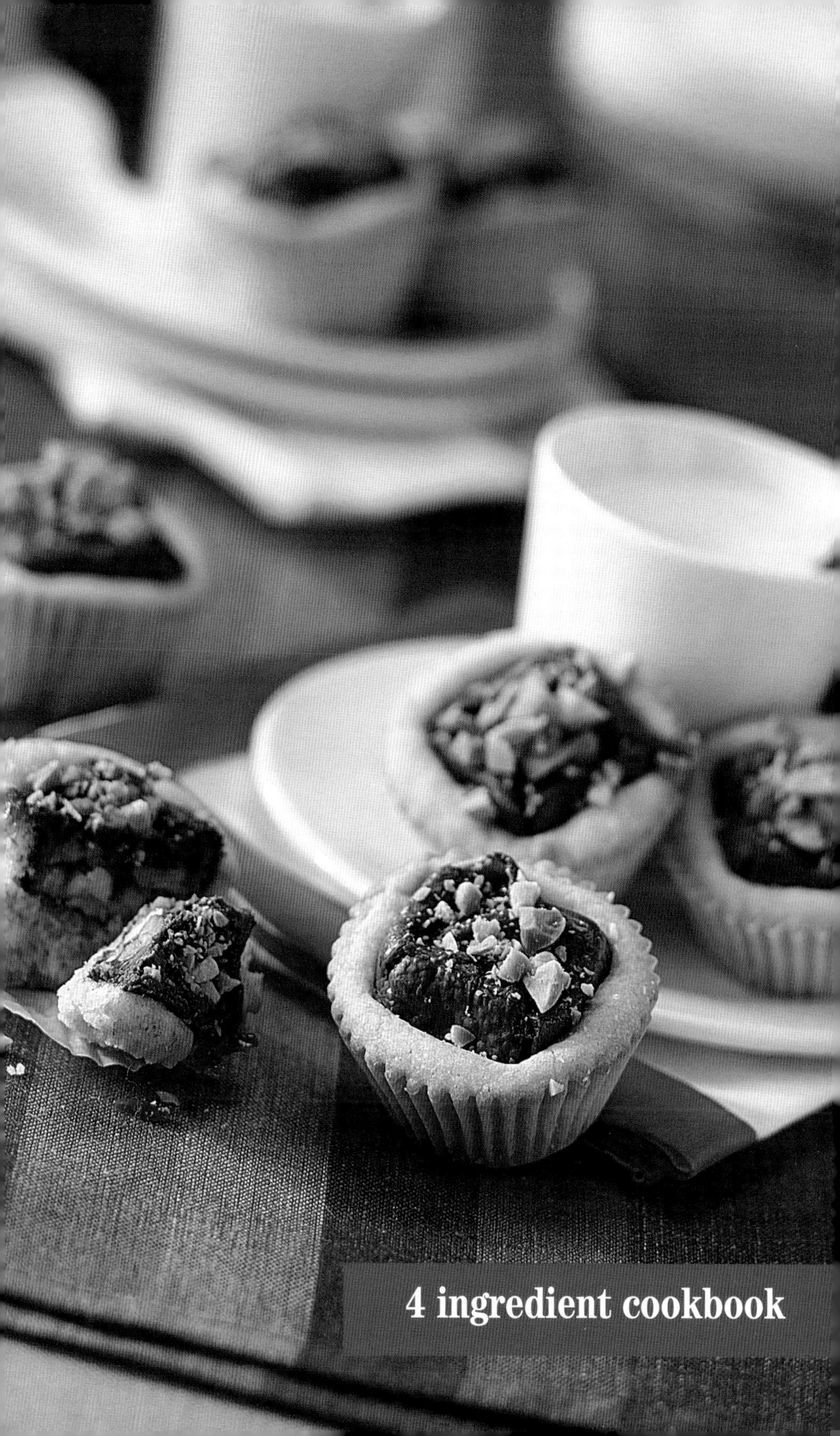
4 ingredient cookbook

Indulgent Desserts

Fluted Kisses® Cups with Peanut Butter Filling

72 HERSHEY'S KISSES® Brand Milk Chocolates, divided
1 cup REESE'S® Creamy Peanut Butter
1 cup powdered sugar
1 tablespoon butter or margarine, softened

1. Line small baking cups (1¾ inches in diameter) with small paper bake cups. Remove wrappers from chocolates.

2. Place 48 chocolates in small microwave-safe bowl. Microwave at HIGH (100%) 1 minute or until chocolate is melted and smooth when stirred. Using small brush, coat inside of paper cups with melted chocolate.

3. Refrigerate 20 minutes; reapply melted chocolate to any thin spots. Refrigerate until firm, preferably overnight. Gently peel paper from chocolate cups.

4. Beat peanut butter, powdered sugar and butter with electric mixer on medium speed in small bowl until smooth. Spoon into chocolate cups. Before serving, top each cup with a chocolate piece. Cover; store cups in refrigerator. *Makes about 2 dozen pieces*

Fluted Kisses® Cups with Peanut Butter Filling

Indulgent Desserts

Dipsy Doodles Butterscotch Dip

**1 (14-ounce) can EAGLE BRAND® Sweetened Condensed
   Milk (NOT evaporated milk)**
1½ cups milk
**1 (4-serving-size) package cook-and-serve butterscotch
   pudding and pie filling mix**
Apples or pears, cored and sliced, or banana chunks

1. In medium saucepan, over medium heat, combine EAGLE BRAND®, milk and pudding mix. Cook and stir until thickened and bubbly; cook 2 minutes more.

2. Cool slightly. Pour into serving bowl or individual cups. Serve warm with fruit.   *Makes about 2½ cups dip*

Tip: Store leftovers covered in the refrigerator. Reheat and serve as a sauce over vanilla ice cream. Sprinkle sauce with miniature semisweet chocolate chips or toasted nuts, if desired.

Prep Time: 15 minutes

Berry-licious Parfait

2 cups lowfat vanilla STONYFIELD FARM® Yogurt
1 cup fresh strawberries, sliced
½ cup fresh blueberries
6 tablespoons granola

Clean and cut the strawberries into quarters, mixing them with the blueberries. Using a tall glass, alternate layers, first beginning with yogurt, then berries, and then yogurt again. Repeat this layering until the glass is full. Top with granola and enjoy.

Makes 2 parfaits

Dipsy Doodles Butterscotch Dip

Special Dark® Fudge Fondue

2 cups (12-ounce package) HERSHEY'S SPECIAL DARK® Chocolate Chips
½ cup light cream
2 teaspoons vanilla extract
Assorted fondue dippers such as marshmallows, cherries, grapes, mandarin orange segments, pineapple chunks, strawberries, slices of other fresh fruits, small pieces of cake, or small brownies

1. Place chocolate chips and light cream in medium microwave-safe bowl. Microwave on HIGH (100%) 1 minute or just until chips are melted and mixture is smooth when stirred. Stir in vanilla.

2. Pour into fondue pot or chafing dish; serve warm with fondue dippers. If mixture thickens, stir in additional light cream, one tablespoon at a time. Refrigerate leftover fondue.

Makes 1½ cups fondue

Stovetop Directions: Combine chocolate chips and light cream in heavy medium saucepan. Cook over low heat, stirring constantly, until chips are melted and mixture is hot. Stir in vanilla, and continue as in Step 2 above.

Special Dark® Fudge Fondue

Indulgent Desserts

Creamy Double Decker Fudge

1 cup REESE'S® Peanut Butter Chips
1 can (14 ounces) sweetened condensed milk (not
**   evaporated milk), divided**
1 teaspoon vanilla extract, divided
1 cup HERSHEY₀'S Semi-Sweet Chocolate Chips

1. Line 8-inch square pan with foil.

2. Place peanut butter chips and ⅔ cup sweetened condensed milk in small microwave-safe bowl. Microwave at HIGH (100%) 1 to 1½ minutes, stirring after 1 minute, until chips are melted and mixture is smooth when stirred. Stir in ½ teaspoon vanilla; spread evenly into prepared pan.

3. Place remaining sweetened condensed milk and chocolate chips in another small microwave-safe bowl; repeat above microwave procedure. Stir in remaining ½ teaspoon vanilla; spread evenly over peanut butter layer.

4. Cover; refrigerate until firm. Remove from pan; place on cutting board. Peel off foil. Cut into squares. Store tightly covered in refrigerator.   *Makes about 4 dozen pieces or 1½ pounds*

Note: For best results, do not double this recipe.

Prep Time: 15 minutes
Cook Time: 3 minutes
Chill Time: 2 hours

Indulgent Desserts

Cinnamon Bubble Ring

¼ cup sugar
½ teaspoon ground cinnamon
1 package (11 ounces) refrigerated French bread dough
1½ tablespoons butter or margarine, melted

1. Preheat oven to 350°F. Spray 9-inch tube pan with nonstick cooking spray. Combine sugar and cinnamon in small bowl.

2. Cut dough into 16 slices; roll into balls. Evenly space 12 balls against outer wall of pan. Arrange remaining 4 balls evenly around inside tube of pan. Brush with butter. Sprinkle sugar mixture evenly over balls.

3. Bake 20 to 25 minutes or until golden brown. Remove to serving plate. Serve warm. *Makes 8 servings*

Prep and Cook Time: 30 minutes

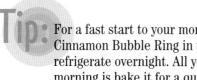

Tip: For a fast start to your morning, prepare the Cinnamon Bubble Ring in the pan, cover and refrigerate overnight. All you have to do in the morning is bake it for a quick, delicious treat.

183

Indulgent Desserts

Rainbow Cakes

> **1 package (18¼ ounces) cake mix (any flavor), plus
>   ingredients to prepare mix**
> **⅓ cup raspberry jam**
> **1 container (16 ounces) vanilla frosting**
>   **Multi-colored coated fruit candies**

1. Prepare cake according to package directions and bake in
17×11-inch jelly-roll pan. Remove from oven; cool completely in
pan on wire rack.

2. Using knife or square cookie cutter, cut 15 (2½ inch) squares
from cake. Spread raspberry jam on one cake layer; top with second
layer. Spread with jam and top with third cake layer.

3. Frost entire cake with vanilla frosting. Repeat to make 5 cakes.
Sprinkle with candies or decorate as desired.   *Makes 5 cakes*

Note: For easy icing application, first brush the crumbs from the
cakes. Then apply a very thin "crumb coating" of icing on the cakes.
Place in the freezer for about 20 minutes, then apply the second,
decorative frosting layer to the top and sides of the cakes.

Rainbow Cake

Indulgent Desserts

Cheesecake Cookie Bars

**2 packages (18 ounces each) refrigerated chocolate chip
  cookie dough, divided**
2 packages (8 ounces each) cream cheese, softened
½ cup sugar
2 eggs

1. Let both doughs stand at room temperature about 15 minutes.
Preheat oven to 350°F. Lightly grease 13×9-inch baking pan.

2. Reserve ¾ of one package of dough. Press remaining
1¼ packages dough evenly onto bottom of prepared pan.

3. Combine cream cheese, sugar and eggs in large bowl; beat until
well blended and smooth. Spread cream cheese mixture over dough
in pan. Break reserved ¾ package of dough into small pieces;
sprinkle over cream cheese mixture.

4. Bake 35 minutes or until center is almost set. Cool completely in
pan on wire rack. Store leftovers covered in refrigerator.

Makes about 2 dozen bars

Cheesecake Cookie Bars

Indulgent Desserts

Black Forest Tarts

1 package (18 ounces) refrigerated triple chocolate cookie dough
⅓ cup unsweetened cocoa powder
1 can (21 ounces) cherry pie filling
3 squares (1 ounce each) white chocolate, finely chopped

1. Let dough stand at room temperature about 15 minutes. Preheat oven to 350°F. Lightly grease 18 standard (2½-inch) muffin pan cups or line with paper or foil baking cups.

2. Combine dough and cocoa in large bowl; beat until well blended. Shape dough into 18 balls; press onto bottoms and up sides of prepared muffin cups.

3. Bake about 15 minutes or until set. Remove from oven; gently press down center of each cookie cup with back of teaspoon. Cool in pan 10 minutes. Remove cups from pans; cool completely on wire rack.

4. Place 1 tablespoon cherry pie filling in each cookie cup.

5. Place white chocolate in small resealable food storage bag. Microwave on MEDIUM (50%) 1 minute; knead bag lightly. Microwave and knead at additional 30-second intervals until white chocolate is completely melted. Cut off tiny corner of bag. Drizzle white chocolate over tarts. Let stand until set.   *Makes 18 tarts*

Black Forest Tart

Indulgent Desserts

S'More Snack Cake

1 package (18¼ ounces) yellow cake mix, plus ingredients to prepare mix
1½ cup bear-shaped graham crackers (honey or chocolate flavor), divided
1 cup chocolate chunks, divided
1½ cups miniature marshmallows

1. Preheat oven to 350°F. Grease 13×9-inch baking pan.

2. Prepare cake mix according to package directions. Spread batter in prepared pan. Sprinkle with ½ cup bears and ½ cup chocolate chunks.

3. Bake 30 minutes. Remove cake from oven; sprinkle with remaining ½ cup chocolate chunks and marshmallows. Arrange remaining 1 cup bears evenly over top of cake as shown in photo.

4. Bake 8 minutes or until marshmallows are golden brown. Cool completely before serving. *Makes 24 servings*

Note: This cake is best served the day it is made.

S'More Snack Cake

Indulgent Desserts

Mint Truffles

1 package (10 ounces) mint chocolate chips
⅓ cup whipping cream
¼ cup (½ stick) butter
1 container (3½ ounces) chocolate sprinkles

1. Line baking sheet with waxed paper; set aside. Melt chips with whipping cream and butter in heavy medium saucepan over low heat, stirring occasionally. Pour into pie pan. Refrigerate until mixture is fudgy, but soft, about 2 hours.

2. Shape about 1 tablespoonful mixture into 1¼-inch ball; place on waxed paper. Repeat procedure with remaining mixture.

3. Place sprinkles in shallow bowl; roll balls in sprinkles. Place truffles in petit four or candy cups. (If sprinkles won't stick because truffle has set, roll truffle between palms until outside is soft.) Truffles may be refrigerated 2 to 3 days or frozen several weeks. *Makes about 24 truffles*

Tip: Truffles can also be coated with unsweetened cocoa, powdered sugar, chopped nuts, colored sprinkles or cookie crumbs to add flavor and prevent the truffle from melting in your fingers.

Table of Contents

Quick Bites & Breads

Mini Chickpea Cakes

1 can (15 ounces) chickpeas, rinsed and drained
1 cup shredded carrots
⅓ cup seasoned dry bread crumbs
¼ cup creamy Italian salad dressing
1 egg

1. Preheat oven to 375°F. Spray baking sheets with nonstick cooking spray.

2. Mash chickpeas coarsely in medium bowl with potato masher. Stir in carrots, bread crumbs, salad dressing and egg; mix well.

3. Shape chickpea mixture into small patties, using about 1 tablespoon mixture for each. Place onto prepared baking sheets.

4. Bake 15 to 18 minutes, turning halfway through baking time, until chickpea cakes are lightly browned on both sides. Serve warm with additional salad dressing for dipping, if desired.

Makes about 2 dozen cakes

Tip: A young child can help with mashing, or scooping the tablespoon to form patties. Substitute your child's favorite flavor of salad dressing, such as ranch dressing, if desired.

Oven-Roasted Asparagus

1 bunch (12 to 14 ounces) asparagus spears
1 tablespoon olive oil
¼ cup shredded Asiago or Parmesan cheese

1. Preheat oven to 425°F.

2. Trim off and discard tough ends of asparagus spears. Peel stem ends with vegetable peeler, if desired. Arrange asparagus in shallow baking dish. Drizzle oil over asparagus; turn stalks to coat. Sprinkle with salt and pepper, if desired.

3. Roast asparagus until tender, about 12 to 18 minutes depending on thickness of asparagus. Chop or leave spears whole. Sprinkle with cheese. *Makes 4 servings*

Quick Spanish Rice

1 cup uncooked white rice
1 cup salsa
1 tablespoon chili powder

Combine 1½ cups water, rice, salsa and chili powder in medium saucepan. Bring to a boil over medium heat. Reduce heat to low; cover and cook 20 minutes or until rice is tender. Serve with sour cream, if desired. *Makes 4 servings*

Oven-Roasted Asparagus

Cauliflower with Onion Butter

1 cup (2 sticks) butter, divided
1 cup diced onion
1 head cauliflower, cut into florets

1. Melt ½ cup butter in 10-inch skillet over medium heat. Add onion; cook and stir until onion is brown, about 20 minutes.

2. Meanwhile, place cauliflower in microwavable container with ½ cup water. Microwave on HIGH 8 minutes or until crisp-tender.

3. Add remaining butter to skillet with onion; cook and stir until butter is melted. Pour over cooked cauliflower; serve immediately.

Makes about 10 servings

Original Ranch® & Cheddar Bread

2 cups (8 ounces) shredded sharp Cheddar cheese
1 cup HIDDEN VALLEY® The Original Ranch® Salad Dressing
1 whole loaf (1 pound) French bread (not sour dough)

Combine cheese and salad dressing in a medium bowl. Cut bread in half lengthwise. Place on a broiler pan and spread dressing mixture evenly over cut side of each half. Broil until lightly brown. Cut each half into 8 pieces.

Makes 16 pieces

Cauliflower with Onion Butter

Parmesan-Pepper Cloverleaf Rolls

¾ cup plus 2 tablespoons shredded Parmesan cheese, divided
½ teaspoon coarsely ground black pepper
1 pound frozen bread dough, thawed

1. Knead ¾ cup cheese and pepper into dough, adding cheese 2 to 3 tablespoons at a time, until evenly mixed throughout. Divide dough equally into 12 pieces; shape into balls. Cover with plastic wrap; let rest 10 minutes.

2. Coat 12 standard (2½-inch) muffin cups and your hands with nonstick cooking spray. Divide each ball of dough into 3 pieces. Roll each piece into small ball. Place 3 balls in each muffin cup. Cover rolls loosely with plastic wrap; let stand in warm place about 30 minutes or until doubled in bulk.

3. Preheat oven to 350°F. Sprinkle rolls with remaining 2 tablespoons cheese. Bake 12 to 15 minutes or until golden brown.

Makes 12 servings

Variation: Grated Parmesan can be used in place of the shredded cheese.

Low-Carb Mashed "Potatoes"

2 heads cauliflower (about 8 cups florets)
1 tablespoon butter
1 tablespoon half-and-half, milk or chicken broth

1. Break cauliflower into equal-size florets. Place in a large saucepan in about 2 inches of water. Simmer over medium heat 20 to 25 minutes, or until cauliflower is very tender and falling apart. (Check occasionally to make sure there is enough water to prevent burning; add water if necessary.) Drain well.

2. Place cooked cauliflower in food processor or blender. Process until almost smooth. Add butter. Process until smooth, adding cream as needed to reach desired consistency. Salt to taste. *Makes 6 servings*

Salsa Macaroni & Cheese

1 jar (1 pound) RAGÚ® Cheesy! Double Cheddar Sauce
1 cup prepared mild salsa
8 ounces elbow macaroni, cooked and drained

1. In 2-quart saucepan, heat Double Cheddar Sauce over medium heat. Stir in salsa; heat through.

2. Toss with hot macaroni. Serve immediately. *Makes 4 servings*

Prep Time: 5 minutes
Cook Time: 15 minutes

Low-Carb Mashed "Potatoes"

Cookie Dough Fun

Peanut Butter & Jelly Pockets

1 package (18 ounces) refrigerated peanut butter cookie dough
1 jar (10 ounces) strawberry or raspberry pastry filling
Coarse decorating sugar

1. Freeze dough 1 hour or until completely firm.

2. Preheat oven to 350°F. Lightly grease cookie sheets.

3. Cut dough into ¼-inch slices; place half of dough slices 2 inches apart on prepared cookie sheets. Spoon about 1 teaspoon pastry filling each onto centers of dough slices; top with remaining dough slices. Sprinkle tops with decorating sugar.

4. Bake 12 to 15 minutes or until edges are light brown. Cool on cookie sheets 3 minutes. Remove to wire racks; cool completely.

Makes about 1½ dozen cookies

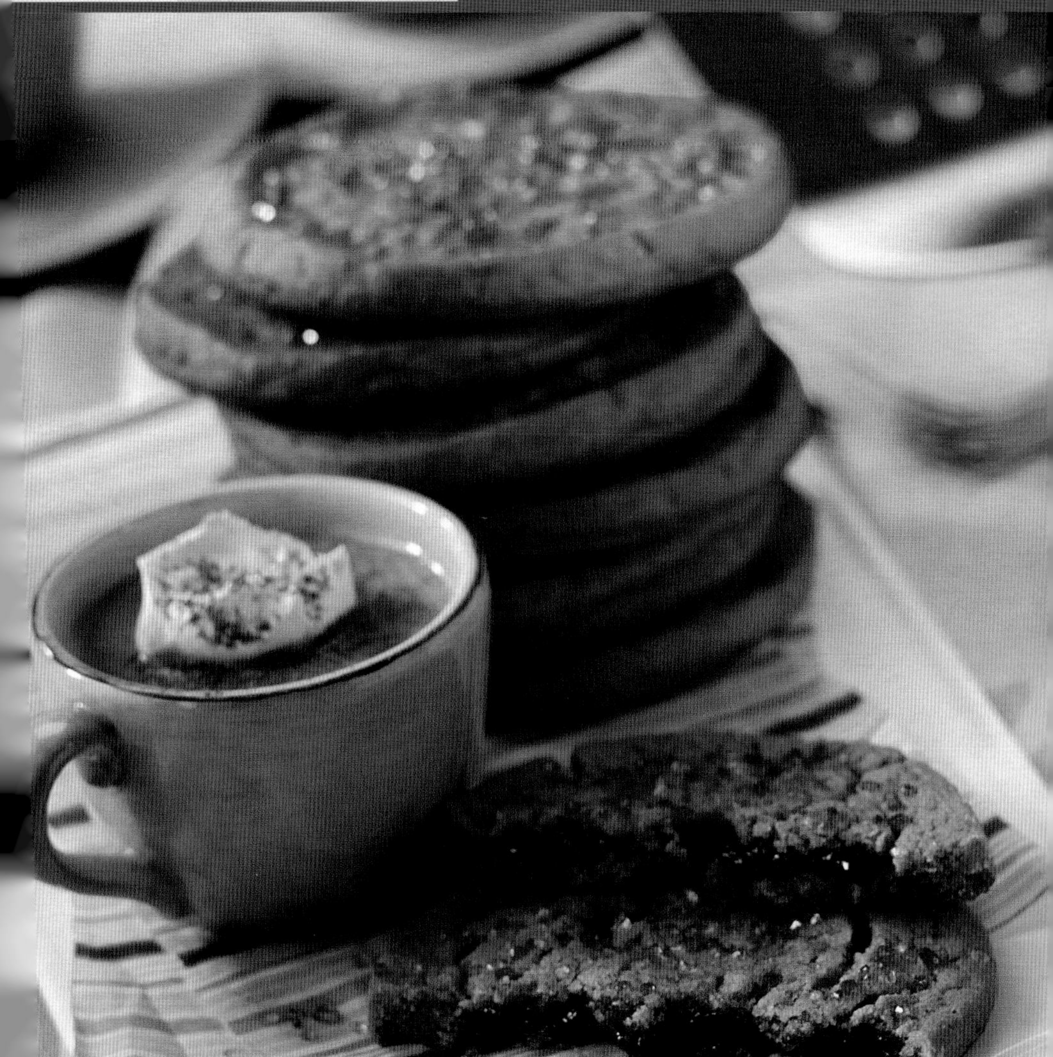

Black & White Bars

1 package (18 ounces) refrigerated sugar cookie dough
1 package (18 ounces) refrigerated triple chocolate
cookie dough
2 squares (1 ounce each) white chocolate, finely chopped

1. Lightly grease 11×7-inch baking pan. Let both packages of dough stand at room temperature about 15 minutes.

2. Preheat oven to 350°F. Press sugar cookie dough evenly onto bottom of prepared pan. Freeze 15 minutes.

3. Press triple chocolate dough evenly over sugar dough in pan. Bake 37 to 40 minutes or until edges are brown and center is set. Cool completely in pan on wire rack.

4. Place white chocolate in small resealable food storage bag. Microwave on MEDIUM (50%) 1 minute; knead bag lightly. Microwave and knead at additional 10-second intervals until white chocolate is completely melted. Cut off tiny corner of bag. Drizzle white chocolate over bars. Let stand until set. *Makes 1 dozen bars*

Tie-Dyed T-Shirts

1 package (18 ounces) refrigerated sugar cookie dough
6 tablespoons all-purpose flour, divided
Red, yellow and blue food coloring

1. Let dough stand at room temperature about 15 minutes.

2. Divide dough into 3 pieces; place in separate medium bowls. Add 2 tablespoons flour and red food coloring to dough in one bowl; beat until well blended and evenly colored. Wrap in plastic wrap; refrigerate 20 minutes. Repeat with second dough piece, 2 tablespoons flour and yellow food coloring. Repeat with remaining dough piece, remaining 2 tablespoons flour and blue food coloring.

3. Preheat oven to 350°F. Lightly grease cookie sheets. Press together 3 dough pieces. Roll dough on lightly floured surface to ¼-inch thickness. Cut dough with 3-inch t-shirt-shaped cookie cutter. Place cutouts 2 inches apart on prepared cookie sheets.

4. Bake 7 to 9 minutes or until firm but not browned. Cool completely on cookie sheets. *Makes about 1½ dozen cookies*

Birthday Cake Cookies

1 package (18 ounces) refrigerated sugar cookie dough
1 container (16 ounces) white frosting
10 small birthday candles

1. Preheat oven to 350°F. Lightly grease 10 mini (1¾-inch) muffin pan cups and 10 standard (2½-inch) muffin pan cups. Shape one-third of dough into 10 (1-inch) balls; press onto bottoms and up sides of prepared mini muffin cups. Shape remaining two-thirds of dough into 10 equal balls; press onto bottoms and up sides of prepared standard muffin cups.

2. Bake mini cookies 8 to 9 minutes or until edges are light brown. Bake regular cookies 10 to 11 minutes or until edges are light brown. Cool 5 minutes in pans on wire racks. Remove cookies to wire racks; cool completely.

3. Add food coloring, if desired, to frosting; mix well. Spread frosting over top and side of each cookie. Place 1 mini cookie on top of 1 regular cookie. Decorate with colored sprinkles or decors, if desired. Press 1 candle into center of each cookie.

Makes 10 cookie cakes

Chocolate Stars

1 package (18 ounces) refrigerated sugar cookie dough in squares or rounds (20 count)
1 tablespoon unsweetened Dutch process cocoa powder
½ cup slivered almonds, toasted* and finely chopped

*To toast almonds, spread in single layer on baking sheet. Bake in preheated 350°F oven 7 to 10 minutes or until golden brown, stirring frequently.

1. Preheat oven to 350°F. Lightly grease cookie sheets. Remove dough from wrapper; let stand at room temperature about 15 minutes.

2. Combine 3 dough squares or rounds and cocoa in medium bowl; beat at medium speed of electric mixer until well blended. Wrap in plastic wrap; refrigerate 20 minutes.

3. Roll chocolate dough on lightly floured surface to ⅛-inch thickness. Cut dough with 1½-inch star cookie cutter; place cutouts 2 inches apart on ungreased cookie sheets. Reroll and cut dough scraps, if necessary to make 18 stars. Bake stars 3 to 5 minutes or until firm but not browned at edges. Cool on cookie sheets 2 minutes. Remove to wire rack; cool completely.

4. Place almonds in shallow bowl. Shape remaining dough squares or rounds into balls; roll in nuts to cover evenly. Place 2 inches apart on prepared cookie sheets. Bake 10 to 12 minutes or until edges are firm and centers are slightly soft. Remove from oven; press one chocolate star cookie into center of each round cookie. Cool on cookie sheets 2 minutes. Remove to wire rack; cool completely.

Makes about 1½ dozen cookies

Thumbprints

**1 package (18 ounces) refrigerated sugar or chocolate
  cookie dough**
All-purpose flour (optional)
¾ cup plus 1 tablespoon fruit preserves, any flavor

1. Grease cookie sheets. Remove dough from wrapper according to package directions. Sprinkle with flour to minimize sticking, if necessary.

2. Cut dough into 26 (1-inch) slices; shape into balls, sprinkling with additional flour, if necessary. Place balls 2 inches apart on prepared cookie sheets. Press deep indentation in center of each ball with thumb. Freeze dough 20 minutes.

3. Preheat oven to 350°F. Bake cookies 12 to 13 minutes or until edges are light golden brown (cookies will have started to puff up and lose their shape). Quickly press down indentation using tip of teaspoon.

4. Return to oven 2 to 3 minutes or until cookies are golden brown and set. Cool cookies completely on cookie sheets. Fill each indentation with about 1½ teaspoons preserves. *Makes 26 cookies*

Tip: These cookies are just as delicious filled with peanut butter or melted semisweet chocolate chips.

Cookie Nuggets

35 butter-flavored round crackers
1 package (18 ounces) refrigerated chocolate chip
cookie dough with peanut butter filling in squares or
rounds (20 count)
Honey and strawberry or raspberry jam

1. Preheat oven to 350°F. Grease cookie sheets. Let dough stand at room temperature about 15 minutes.

2. Meanwhile, place crackers in resealable food storage bag; seal bag. Crush crackers with rolling pin until fine crumbs form. Reserve ½ cup crumbs.

3. Combine dough and remaining crumbs in large bowl; beat at medium speed of electric mixer until well blended. Shape 2 rounded teaspoonfuls of dough into oval; flatten slightly. Roll in reserved crumbs; place on prepared cookie sheets. Pinch in sides of oval to make cookie resemble chicken nugget. Repeat with remaining dough and crumbs.

4. Bake 8 to 10 minutes or until set. Cool on cookie sheets 10 minutes. Remove to wire racks; cool completely.

5. Serve cookies with honey and jam for dipping.

Makes about 2½ dozen cookies

Tip: If dough becomes too soft to shape, refrigerate 15 minutes.

Cookie Nuggets

Pretty Posies

1 package (18 ounces) refrigerated sugar cookie dough
Orange and blue or purple food coloring
1 tablespoon colored sprinkles

1. Let dough stand at room temperature about 15 minutes.

2. Combine ⅙ of dough, orange food coloring and sprinkles in small bowl; beat until well blended. Shape into 7½-inch-long log. Wrap in plastic wrap; refrigerate 30 minutes or until firm.

3. Combine remaining dough and blue food coloring in large bowl; beat until well blended. Shape dough into disc. Wrap in plastic wrap; refrigerate 30 minutes or until firm.

4. Roll out blue dough between sheets of waxed paper into 7½×6-inch rectangle. Remove top sheet of waxed paper. Place orange log in center of blue rectangle. Fold blue edges up and around orange log; press seam together. Roll gently to form smooth log. Wrap waxed paper around dough; twist ends to secure. Freeze log 20 minutes.

5. Preheat oven to 350°F. Lightly grease cookie sheets. Cut log into ¼-inch slices. Place 2 inches apart on prepared cookie sheets. Using 2½-inch flower-shaped cookie cutter, cut slices into flowers; remove and discard dough scraps.

6. Bake 15 to 17 minutes or until edges are lightly browned. Remove to wire racks; cool completely. *Makes about 1½ dozen cookies*

Toffee Chipsters

1 package (18 ounces) refrigerated sugar cookie dough
1 cup white chocolate chips
1 bag (8 ounces) chocolate-covered toffee baking bits, divided

1. Preheat oven to 350°F. Lightly grease cookie sheets. Let dough stand at room temperature about 15 minutes.

2. Combine dough, white chocolate chips and 1 cup toffee bits in large bowl; beat until well blended. Drop dough by rounded tablespoonfuls 2 inches apart onto prepared cookie sheets. Press remaining ⅓ cup toffee bits into dough mounds.

3. Bake 10 to 12 minutes or until set. Cool on cookie sheets 1 minute. Remove to wire racks; cool completely. *Makes about 2 dozen cookies*

tip

Freeze baked cookies in airtight containers or freezer bags for up to six months. Thaw cookies and brownies unwrapped at room temperature.

Toffee Chipsters

Sweet Treats

Tiger Stripes

1 package (12 ounces) semisweet chocolate chips
3 tablespoons creamy or chunky peanut butter, divided
2 (2-ounce) white chocolate baking bars

1. Line 8-inch square pan with foil; lightly grease foil. Melt semisweet chocolate and 2 tablespoons peanut butter in small saucepan over low heat; stir until melted and smooth. Pour chocolate mixture into prepared pan. Let stand 10 to 15 minutes to cool slightly.

2. Melt white chocolate and remaining 1 tablespoon peanut butter in small saucepan over low heat. Drop spoonfuls of white chocolate mixture over semisweet chocolate mixture in pan.

3. Using small metal spatula or knife, swirl chocolates to create tiger stripes. Freeze about 1 hour or until firm. Remove from pan; peel off foil. Cut or break into pieces. Refrigerate until ready to serve.

Makes about 3 dozen pieces

Reese's® Haystacks

1⅔ cups (10-ounce package) REESE'S® Peanut Butter Chips
1 tablespoon shortening (do *not* use butter, margarine,
   spread or oil)
2½ cups (5-ounce can) chow mein noodles

1. Line tray with wax paper.

2. Place peanut butter chips and shortening in medium microwave-safe bowl. Microwave at HIGH (100%) 1 minute; stir. If necessary, microwave at HIGH an additional 15 seconds at a time, stirring after each heating, just until chips are melted and mixture is smooth when stirred. Immediately add chow mein noodles; stir to coat.

3. Drop mixture by heaping teaspoons onto prepared tray or into paper candy cups. Let stand until firm. If necessary, cover and refrigerate several minutes until firm. Store in tightly covered container. *Makes about 2 dozen treats*

Sugar-and-Spice Twists

1 tablespoon granulated sugar
¼ teaspoon ground cinnamon
1 package (6-count) refrigerated breadsticks

1. Preheat oven to 350°F. Spray baking sheet with nonstick cooking spray; set aside.

2. Combine sugar and cinnamon in shallow dish or plate. Divide breadstick dough into 6 pieces. Roll each piece into 12-inch rope. Roll in sugar-cinnamon mixture. Twist into pretzel shape. Place on prepared baking sheet.

3. Bake 15 to 18 minutes or until lightly browned. Remove from baking sheet. Cool 5 minutes. Serve warm.   *Makes 6 servings*

tip

Use colored sugar sprinkles in place of the granulated sugar in this recipe for a fun "twist" of color that's perfect for holidays, birthdays or simple everyday celebrations.

Dessert Grape Clusters

2 pounds seedless red and/or green grapes
1 pound premium white chocolate, coarsely chopped
2 cups finely chopped honey-roasted cashews

1. Rinse grapes under cold running water in colander; drain well. Cut grapes into clusters of 3 grapes. Place clusters in single layer on paper towels. Let stand at room temperature until completely dry.

2. Melt white chocolate in top of double boiler over hot, not boiling, water. Stir until white chocolate is melted. Remove from heat.

3. Place cashews in shallow bowl. Working with 1 cluster at a time, holding by stem, dip grapes into melted chocolate; allow excess to drain back into pan. Roll grapes gently in cashews. Place grapes, stem sides up, on waxed paper; repeat with remaining clusters. Refrigerate until firm. Serve within 4 hours.

Makes about 3 dozen clusters

Quick Holiday Raspberry Fudge

3⅓ cups HERSHEY₀S Semi-Sweet Chocolate Chips
1 can (14 ounces) sweetened condensed milk (not evaporated milk)
1½ teaspoons raspberry-flavored liqueur or raspberry extract

1. Line 8-inch square pan with foil, extending foil over edges of pan.

2. Place chocolate chips and sweetened condensed milk in medium microwave-safe bowl. Microwave at HIGH (100%) 1 minute; stir. If necessary, microwave an additional 30 seconds at a time, stirring after each heating, just until chips are melted and mixture is smooth when stirred; stir in liqueur. Spread evenly into prepared pan.

3. Cover; refrigerate 2 hours or until firm. Remove from pan; place on cutting board. Peel off foil; cut into squares. Store loosely covered at room temperature. *Makes about 4 dozen pieces*

Note: For best results, do not double this recipe.

Prep Time: 5 minutes
Cook Time: 1 minute
Chill Time: 2 hours

Dulce De Leche Dessert Sandwiches

1 pint (2 cups) Dulce de Leche ice cream
¾ cup pecans
12 chocolate cookies

1. Preheat oven to 350°F.

2. Remove ice cream from freezer; let stand at room temperature 10 minutes or until slightly softened.

3. Place pecans in single layer in a shallow baking pan. Bake 8 minutes or until golden and fragrant; set aside to cool. Finely chop pecans; reserve.

4. Spread ⅓ cup ice cream onto flat sides of half the cookies. Place remaining cookies, flat sides down, on ice cream; press cookies together lightly. Use a spatula to smooth or remove excess ice cream, if necessary. Wrap each sandwich individually in plastic wrap; freeze 30 minutes or until firm.

5. Coat ice cream edges with pecans; rewrap in plastic. Freeze an additional 30 minutes.   *Makes 6 servings*

Note: Ice cream sandwiches should be eaten within three days. After three days, cookies will absorb moisture and become soggy.

Chocolate Peanut Butter
Ice Cream Sandwiches

2 tablespoons creamy peanut butter
8 chocolate wafer cookies
⅔ cup vanilla ice cream, softened

1. Spread peanut butter over flat sides of all cookies.

2. Spoon ice cream over peanut butter on 4 cookies. Top with remaining 4 cookies, peanut butter sides down. Press down lightly to force ice cream to edges of sandwiches.

3. Wrap each sandwich tightly in foil. Freeze at least 2 hours or up to 5 days.

Makes 4 servings

tip

Try this recipe with your favorite ice cream flavor. Press miniature chocolate chips or finely chopped nuts to the sides for a fun addition.

Chocolate Peanut Butter Ice Cream Sandwiches

Double Peanut Clusters

1⅔ cups (10-ounce package) REESE'S® Peanut Butter Chips
1 tablespoon shortening (do not use butter, margarine,
spread or oil)
2 cups salted peanuts

1. Line cookie sheet with wax paper.

2. Place peanut butter chips and shortening in large microwave-safe bowl. Microwave at HIGH (100%) 1½ minutes; stir until chips are melted and mixture is smooth. If necessary, microwave an additional 30 seconds until chips are melted when stirred. Stir in peanuts.

3. Drop by rounded teaspoons onto prepared cookie sheet. (Mixture may also be dropped into small paper candy cups.) Cool until set. Store in cool, dry place.   *Makes about 2½ dozen clusters*

Butterscotch Nut Clusters: Follow above directions, substituting 1¾ cups (11-ounce package) HERSHEY'S Butterscotch Chips for Peanut Butter Chips.

Double Peanut Clusters

Chocolate-Dipped Strawberries

2 cups (11½ ounces) milk chocolate chips
1 tablespoon shortening
12 large strawberries with stems, rinsed and dried

1. Line baking sheet with waxed paper; set aside.

2. Melt chips with shortening in top of double boiler over hot, not boiling, water, stirring constantly.

3. Dip about half of each strawberry in chocolate. Remove excess chocolate by scraping bottom of strawberry across rim of pan. Place strawberries on prepared baking sheet. Let stand until set.

4. Store in refrigerator in container between layers of waxed paper.

Makes about 12 strawberries

Variation: Melt 8 ounces white chocolate or pastel confectionery coating. Redip dipped strawberries; leave a portion of the milk chocolate coating showing.

Hint: Stir chopped dried fruits, raisins or nuts into remaining chocolate; drop by tablespoonfuls onto a baking sheet lined with waxed paper.

Chocolate-Dipped Strawberries

Sinfully Simple Chocolate Cake

**1 package (18¼ ounces) chocolate cake mix plus
ingredients to prepare mix
1 cup whipping cream, chilled
⅓ cup chocolate syrup**

1. Prepare cake mix according to package directions. Pour into prepared 17×11-inch jelly roll pan. Bake 20 minutes or until toothpick inserted comes out clean.

2. Beat whipping cream with electric mixer at high speed until it begins to thicken. Gradually add chocolate syrup; continue beating until soft peaks form.

3. Using a ruler or square cookie cutters, cut 10 each 3-inch squares, 2-inch squares and 1-inch squares. Place 1 (3-inch) square on serving plate. Spread with frosting. Top with 2-inch square. Spread frosting and top with 1-inch square. Frost sides and top of cake. Repeat to form 10 cakes. Store tightly covered at room temperature.

Simple Chocolate Curls: Place an 8-ounce chocolate bar on waxed paper. Place on top of refrigerator, by a sunny window, or anywhere between 80°F and 85°F for about 30 minutes to slightly soften. Find the flattest side of the chocolate bar and using long strokes, pull a vegetable peeler towards you to create curls. Refrigerate curls until needed for decorating. Use a toothpick to transfer curls to cake.

Sinfully Simple Chocolate Cake

Easy Raspberry Ice Cream

1¾ cups frozen unsweetened raspberries
2 to 3 tablespoons powdered sugar
½ cup whipping cream

1. Place raspberries in food processor fitted with steel blade. Process using on/off pulses about 15 seconds or until raspberries are evenly chopped.

2. Add sugar; process using on/off pulses until smooth. With processor running, add cream; process until well blended. Serve immediately.   *Makes 3 servings*

tip

This recipe works great with other fruits as well. Try strawberries, blueberries or peaches.

Cinnamon Apple Chips

2 cups unsweetened apple juice
1 cinnamon stick
2 Washington Red Delicious apples

1. In large skillet or saucepan, combine apple juice and cinnamon stick; bring to a low boil while preparing apples.

2. With paring knife, slice off ½ inch from tops and bottoms of apples and discard (or eat). Stand apples on either cut end; cut crosswise into ⅛-inch-thick slices, rotating apple as necessary to cut even slices.

3. Drop slices into boiling juice; cook 4 to 5 minutes or until slices appear translucent and lightly golden. Meanwhile, preheat oven to 250°F.

4. With slotted spatula, remove apple slices from juice and pat dry. Arrange slices on wire racks, making sure none overlap. Place racks on middle shelf in oven; bake 30 to 40 minutes until slices are lightly browned and almost dry to touch. Let chips cool on racks completely before storing in airtight container. *Makes about 40 chips*

Tip: There is no need to core apples because boiling in juice for several minutes softens core and removes seeds.

Favorite recipe from *Washington Apple Commission*

5 ingredient cookbook

Quick Bites & Breads

Pepperoni-Oregano Focaccia

1 tablespoon cornmeal
1 can (10 ounces) refrigerated pizza dough
½ cup finely chopped pepperoni
1½ teaspoons finely chopped fresh oregano *or* ½ teaspoon dried oregano
2 teaspoons olive oil

1. Preheat oven to 425°F. Grease large baking sheet; sprinkle with cornmeal. Set aside.

2. Unroll dough onto lightly floured surface. Pat dough into 12×9-inch rectangle. Sprinkle half the pepperoni and half the oregano over one side of dough. Fold over dough, making 12×4½-inch rectangle.

3. Roll dough into 12×9-inch rectangle. Place on prepared baking sheet. Prick dough with fork at 2-inch intervals about 30 times. Brush with oil; sprinkle with remaining pepperoni and oregano.

4. Bake 12 to 15 minutes or until golden brown. (Prick dough several more times if dough puffs as it bakes.) Cut into strips.

Makes 12 servings

Tangy Cheese Dip

1 container (8 ounces) whipped cream cheese
¼ cup milk
3 tablespoons *French's*® Spicy Brown Mustard or *French's*® Honey Mustard
2 tablespoons mayonnaise
2 tablespoons minced green onions

1. Combine all ingredients; mix until well blended.

2. Serve with vegetables or chips. *Makes 5 (¼-cup) servings*

Prep Time: 15 minutes

Quick Bites & Breads

Hot Molten Blobs

1 can (12 ounces) refrigerated buttermilk biscuits
2 tablespoons mayonnaise
1½ tablespoons honey mustard
12 (¾-inch) ham cubes
36 (¾-inch) Cheddar cheese cubes

1. Preheat oven to 400°F. Place sheet of aluminum foil on oven rack.

2. Coat 10 standard (2½-inch) muffin pan cups with nonstick cooking spray and set aside. Place biscuit in each pan cup.

3. In a small bowl, combine mayonnaise and mustard. Stir until well blended.

4. Using thumbs, press down to make a deep indentation in each of the biscuits. Spoon equal amounts of mayonnaise mixture into biscuits. Top each with 1 ham cube and 3 cheese cubes.

5. Place muffin pan on prepared oven rack. Bake about 12 minutes or until biscuits are golden, puffed slightly and overflowing with cheese.

6. Remove from oven and let stand 3 minutes before removing from pans. Serve hot. *Makes 10 blobs*

tip: Serve blobs with scrambled eggs and orange juice for a fun, yet complete breakfast.

Quick Bites & Breads

Wild Wedges

2 (8-inch) flour tortillas
⅓ cup shredded Cheddar cheese
⅓ cup chopped cooked chicken or turkey
1 green onion, thinly sliced
2 tablespoons mild thick and chunky salsa

1. Heat large nonstick skillet over medium heat until hot.

2. Spray one side of one flour tortilla with nonstick cooking spray; place, sprayed side down, in skillet. Top with cheese, chicken, green onion and salsa. Place remaining tortilla over mixture; spray with cooking spray.

3. Cook 2 to 3 minutes per side or until golden brown and cheese is melted. Cut into 8 triangles. *Makes 4 servings*

Variation: For bean quesadillas, omit the chicken and spread ⅓ cup canned refried beans over one of the tortillas.

Melted Brie & Artichoke Dip

1 envelope KNORR® Recipe Classics™ Spring Vegetable Soup, Dip and Recipe Mix
1 can (14 ounces) artichoke hearts, drained and chopped
1 cup Hellmann's® or Best Foods® Real Mayonnaise
1 container (8 ounces) sour cream
8 ounces Brie cheese, rind removed and cut into chunks

Preheat oven to 350°F. In 1-quart casserole, combine all ingredients.

Bake uncovered 30 minutes or until heated through.

Serve with sliced French bread or your favorite dippers.

Makes 3 cups dip

Prep Time: 10 minutes
Cook Time: 30 minutes

Quick Bites & Breads

Ham and Cheese "Sushi" Rolls

4 thin slices deli ham (about 4×4 inches)
1 package (8 ounces) cream cheese, softened
1 piece (4 inches long) seedless cucumber, quartered
    lengthwise (about ½ cucumber)
4 thin slices (about 4×4 inches) American or Cheddar
    cheese, at room temperature
1 red bell pepper, cut into thin 4-inch-long strips

1. For ham sushi, pat 1 ham slice with paper towel to remove excess moisture. Spread 2 tablespoons cream cheese to edges of ham slice. Pat 1 cucumber piece with paper towel to remove excess moisture; place at edge of ham slice. Roll up tightly, pressing gently to seal. Wrap in plastic wrap; refrigerate. Repeat with remaining ham slices, cream cheese and cucumber pieces.

2. For cheese sushi, spread 2 tablespoons cream cheese to edges of 1 cheese slice. Place 2 strips red pepper at edge of cheese slice. Roll up tightly, pressing gently to seal. Wrap in plastic wrap; refrigerate. Repeat with remaining cheese slices, cream cheese and red pepper strips.

3. To serve, remove plastic wrap from ham and cheese rolls. Cut each roll into 8 (½-inch-wide) pieces.   *Makes 8 servings*

Nacho Popcorn

3 quarts popped JOLLY TIME® Pop Corn
2 cups corn chips
¼ cup butter or margarine
1½ teaspoons Mexican seasoning
¾ cup shredded taco cheese

Preheat oven to 300°F. Spread popped popcorn and corn chips in shallow baking pan lined with foil. Melt butter in small pan. Stir in Mexican seasoning. Pour over popcorn mixture and toss well. Sprinkle with cheese and toss to mix. Bake 5 to 7 minutes or until cheese is melted. Serve immediately.   *Makes about 3½ quarts*

Can't Get Enough Chicken Wings

18 chicken wings (about 3 pounds)
1 envelope LIPTON® RECIPE SECRETS® Savory Herb with Garlic Soup Mix
½ cup water
2 to 3 tablespoons hot pepper sauce* (optional)
2 tablespoons margarine or butter

*Use more or less hot pepper sauce as desired.

1. Cut tips off chicken wings (save tips for soup). Cut chicken wings in half at joint. Deep fry, bake or broil until golden brown and crunchy.

2. Meanwhile, in small saucepan, combine soup mix, water and hot pepper sauce. Cook over low heat, stirring occasionally, 2 minutes or until thickened. Remove from heat and stir in margarine.

3. In large bowl, toss cooked chicken wings with hot soup mixture until evenly coated. Serve, if desired, over greens with cut-up celery.

Makes 36 appetizers

Colorful Kabobs

30 cocktail-size smoked sausages
10 to 20 cherry tomatoes
10 to 20 large pimiento-stuffed green olives
2 yellow bell peppers, cut into 1-inch squares
¼ cup butter or margarine, melted

1. Preheat oven to 450°F.

2. Thread sausages, tomatoes, olives and bell peppers onto wooden skewers*.

3. Place skewers on rack in shallow baking pan. Brush with melted butter. Bake 4 to 6 minutes until hot.   *Makes 10 kabobs*

*Soak skewers in water 20 minutes before using to prevent burning.

Quick Bites & Breads

Grilled Eggplant Roll-Ups

¼ cup (2 ounces) hummus
2 slices grilled eggplant
½ cup (2 ounce) crumbled feta cheese
½ cup chopped green onions
2 fresh tomato slices

Spread hummus on grilled eggplant slices. Top with feta, scallions and tomato. Roll tightly. *Makes 2 servings*

Sesame Italian Breadsticks

¼ cup (1 ounce) grated Parmesan cheese
3 tablespoons sesame seeds
2 teaspoons dried Italian seasoning
12 frozen bread dough dinner rolls, thawed
¼ cup (½ stick) butter, melted

1. Preheat oven to 425°F. Spray large baking sheet with nonstick cooking spray.

2. Combine cheese, sesame seeds, Italian seasoning and 1 teaspoon salt, if desired, in small bowl. Spread onto shallow plate.

3. Roll each dinner roll into rope, about 8 inches long and ½ inch thick, on lightly floured surface; place on baking sheet. Brush tops and sides with butter. Roll each buttered rope in cheese mixture, pressing mixture into dough. Return ropes to baking sheet, placing 2 inches apart. Twist each rope 3 times. Press both ends of rope down on baking sheet. Bake 10 to 12 minutes or until golden brown.

Makes 12 breadsticks

Quick Bites & Breads

Chicken Tenders in Bacon Blankets

¼ cup Dijon mustard
¼ cup maple syrup
¼ teaspoon chili powder
4 chicken breast tenders, cut in half lengthwise
(about 12 ounces)
8 bacon strips

1. Preheat broiler. Combine mustard, maple syrup and chili powder in medium bowl. Reserve half mustard mixture. Brush each chicken tender with remaining mustard mixture. Wrap 1 bacon strip around each chicken tender.

2. Place chicken tenders, bacon ends down, on rack of broiler pan. Broil 5 inches from heat 4 to 5 minutes on each side or until bacon is crisp and chicken is no longer pink in center. Serve with reserved mustard mixture for dipping.   *Makes 4 servings*

BelGioioso® Asiago-Mayo Bread

1 (1-pound) loaf unsliced Italian bread
½ cup shredded BELGIOIOSO® Asiago Cheese
½ cup mayonnaise
2 tablespoons chopped chives
¼ teaspoon garlic powder

Preheat broiler. Cut bread crosswise in half. In small bowl, stir together BelGioioso Asiago Cheese, mayonnaise, chives and garlic powder. Spread mixture on bread pieces. Broil 2 to 3 minutes or until light brown. Serve immediately.   *Makes 8 to 12 servings*

Quick Bites & Breads

Chipotle Chili Hummus Dip

½ cup *French's® Gourmayo™* Smoked Chipotle Light
    Mayonnaise
½ cup prepared hummus dip
1 tablespoon *Frank's® RedHot® Chile 'n Lime™* Hot Sauce or
    Frank's® RedHot® Cayenne Pepper Sauce
1 tablespoon minced green onion
½ teaspoon finely minced garlic

1. Combine all ingredients in small bowl until blended. Chill.

2. Serve with cut-up vegetables or chips.

Makes about 4 (¼-cup) servings

Tip: Use as a spread on sandwiches or wraps.

Prep Time: 5 minutes

Pizza Bianca

1 pound white or whole-wheat pizza dough
2 tablespoons olive oil, plus more to brush baking sheet
2 teaspoons minced garlic
2 cups grated CABOT® Sharp Cheddar (about 8 ounces)
2 tablespoons coarsely chopped fresh rosemary leaves or
    ¼ cup torn fresh basil leaves

1. Place rack in lower third of oven and preheat oven to 450°F.
Brush large baking sheet generously with oil.

2. On floured work surface, roll dough out into rectangle the size of
baking sheet, letting it rest for several minutes if it becomes too
springy to work with. Transfer to prepared baking sheet.

3. In small skillet, heat oil over medium heat; add garlic and cook,
stirring, until garlic is fragrant and just beginning to color, about
1 minute. Immediately brush mixture all over top of dough.

4. Sprinkle with cheese and scatter rosemary or basil on top. Bake
for 12-15 minutes, or until golden on top and browned underneath.
Serve hot or at room temperature. *Makes 4 servings*

Quick Bites & Breads

Chavrie® Quesadilla

½ cup drained cooked black beans
½ cup drained chunky tomato salsa
6 (6-inch) flour tortillas
1 (5.3-ounce) package CHAVRIE®, Plain or Basil & Roasted Garlic
2 teaspoons olive oil

Combine black beans and salsa; spread onto 3 tortillas.

Lightly toast remaining 3 tortillas in oiled skillet.

Spread Chavrie onto toasted tortillas in skillet; place on top of black bean mixture to make "sandwich."

Add olive oil to skillet. Heat quesadillas in skillet over medium heat until cheese starts to soften and tortilla starts to brown. Serve as is or cut into wedges. *Makes 6 servings*

Italian Pull-Aparts

1 pound frozen bread dough, thawed but cold
1 egg, lightly beaten
1½ tablespoons butter or margarine, melted
½ teaspoon dried Italian seasoning
¼ teaspoon garlic powder

Cut dough into 12 slices; cut each slice into 4 pieces. In medium bowl, mix egg, butter, Italian seasoning and garlic powder. Add a few pieces of dough at a time, coating all sides; remove pieces with slotted spoon and place in 8×3×3-inch pan coated with nonstick cooking spray. Continue until all pieces are coated. Pour rest of egg mixture over dough pieces.

Cover with plastic wrap and let rise until doubled, about 1 hour. Bake at 350°F for 30 to 35 minutes or until golden brown.
Makes 12 servings

Favorite recipe from **North Dakota Wheat Commission**

Sandwiches & Salad

Mild Curry Chicken Salad with Fruit

2 cups (1 pint) prepared deli creamy chicken salad
2 teaspoons granulated sugar
1½ to 2 teaspoons curry powder or to taste
⅛ teaspoon cayenne pepper
8 fresh pineapple chunks

1. Combine chicken salad, sugar, curry powder and cayenne pepper in medium bowl. Stir gently to blend thoroughly.

2. Arrange pineapple chunks on 4 individual plates. Spoon equal amounts salad on top of pineapple.   *Makes 4 servings*

Note: The curry flavor in this dish is mild, so adjust it for your taste before serving.

Variation: Add 2 tablespoons *each* currants, chopped apples, sliced red grapes, sliced green onions, and/or toasted, slivered almonds. Serve on a bed of spring greens or baby spinach leaves. Garnish with fresh pineapple chunks.

Cook's Tip: Some find the taste of curry harsh and prefer it cooked or toasted. To toast, heat a dry, nonstick skillet over medium-high heat until hot, add curry and stir or tilt pan constantly to prevent burning. Cook just until fully flavorful, about 1 minute. Immediately remove from skillet.

5 ingredient cookbook

Sandwiches & Salad

Havarti & Onion Sandwiches

1½ teaspoons olive oil
⅓ cup thinly sliced red onion
4 slices pumpernickel bread
6 ounces dill havarti cheese, cut into slices
½ cup prepared coleslaw

1. Heat olive oil in large nonstick skillet over medium heat until hot. Add onion; cook and stir 5 minutes or until tender. Layer 2 bread slices with onion, cheese and coleslaw; top with remaining 2 bread slices.

2. Place same skillet or large grill pan over medium heat until hot. Add sandwiches; press down lightly with spatula or weigh down with small plate. Cook sandwiches 4 to 5 minutes per side or until cheese melts and sandwiches are toasted. *Makes 2 sandwiches*

Sweet & Tasty Hawaiian Sandwich

½ cup pineapple preserves
1 tablespoon Dijon mustard
1 round loaf (16 ounces) Hawaiian bread
8 ounces brick cheese, thinly sliced
8 ounces thinly sliced deli ham

1. Combine preserves and mustard in small bowl; mix well. Cut bread in half horizontally. Pull out and discard center from bread top, leaving 1-inch shell. Spread preserves mixture on bottom half of bread. Layer with cheese and ham; close sandwich with top half of bread. Spray outsides of sandwich lightly with nonstick cooking spray.

2. Place large nonstick skillet over medium heat until hot. Add sandwich; press down lightly with spatula or weigh down with small plate. Cook sandwich 4 to 5 minutes per side or until cheese melts and sandwich is golden brown. Cut into wedges; garnish with green olives, if desired. *Makes 4 to 6 servings*

Sandwiches & Salad

Ragú® Pizza Burgers

1 pound ground beef
2 cups RAGÚ® Old World Style® Pasta Sauce, divided
1 cup shredded mozzarella cheese (about 4 ounces), divided
¼ teaspoon salt
6 English muffins, split and toasted

1. In small bowl, combine ground beef, ½ cup Ragú Pasta Sauce, ½ cup cheese and salt. Shape into 6 patties. Grill or broil until done.

2. Meanwhile, heat remaining pasta sauce. To serve, arrange burgers on muffin halves. Top with remaining cheese, sauce and muffin halves. *Makes 6 servings*

Prep Time: 10 minutes
Cook Time: 15 minutes

Chicken Caesar

1 package (about 1 pound) PERDUE® Seasoned Boneless Chicken Breast, Lemon Pepper
1 head Romaine lettuce, washed and torn into pieces
½ cup prepared Caesar salad dressing, divided
2 ripe tomatoes, cut into wedges
1 cup Caesar-seasoned croutons

Prepare outdoor grill for cooking or preheat broiler. Grill or broil breasts 6 to 8 inches from heat source 6 to 8 minutes per side, until cooked through. Toss lettuce with ⅓ cup salad dressing. Slice chicken and serve warm on bed of lettuce; garnish with tomato slices and top with croutons. Before serving, drizzle with additional dressing. *Makes 4 servings*

Prep Time: 10 minutes
Cook Time: 15 minutes

Sandwiches & Salad

BLT Pizza Wedges

12 slices JENNIE-O STORE® Turkey Bacon
⅓ cup mayonnaise
4 (6-inch) pre-baked Italian pizza shells
2 Roma tomatoes, thinly sliced
1 cup lettuce, shredded

Heat oven to 450°F. Cook bacon according to package directions. Spread mayonnaise on each pizza shell. Top with sliced tomatoes and bacon. Place on baking sheet. Bake 8 to 10 minutes or until hot. Sprinkle with shredded lettuce. Cut into wedges.

Makes 4 servings

Tropical Turkey Melt

1 English muffin, split
1 teaspoon Dijon mustard
3 slices (about 3 ounces) lean deli smoked turkey
3 thin slices papaya
1 slice (1 ounce) Monterey Jack cheese

1. Spread inside of muffin halves with mustard. On one half, layer turkey, papaya and cheese. Press remaining muffin half, mustard-side down, over cheese.

2. Spray small skillet with butter-flavored cooking spray. Lightly spread butter over surface of muffins, if desired. Cook sandwich over medium heat until lightly toasted, about 4 minutes; turn and cook on other side until lightly toasted and cheese is melted. Serve hot.

Makes 1 serving

Thai-Style Warm Noodle Salad

8 ounces uncooked angel hair pasta
½ cup chunky peanut butter
¼ cup soy sauce
2 green onions, thinly sliced
1 carrot, shredded

1. Cook pasta according to package directions.

2. Meanwhile, blend peanut butter and soy sauce in serving bowl until smooth.

3. Drain pasta, reserving 5 tablespoons water. Mix hot pasta water with peanut butter mixture until smooth; toss pasta with sauce. Stir in green onions and carrot. Sprinkle with red pepper flakes, if desired. Serve warm or at room temperature. *Makes 4 servings*

Note: You can make this salad into a heartier meal by mixing in any leftover cooked chicken or beef.

Prep and Cook Time: 12 minutes

tip: This salad is as versatile as it is easy to make. It can be prepared a day ahead and served warm or cold—perfect for potlucks, picnics and even lunch boxes.

Sandwiches & Salad

Bacon & Tomato Melts

4 slices cooked bacon
4 slices (1 ounce each) Cheddar cheese
1 tomato, sliced
4 slices whole wheat bread
  Butter, melted

1. Layer 2 slices bacon, 2 slices cheese and sliced tomato each on 2 bread slices; top with remaining bread slices. Brush outsides of sandwiches with butter.

2. Place large grill pan or skillet over medium heat until hot. Add sandwiches; press down lightly with spatula or weigh down with small plate. Cook sandwiches 4 to 5 minutes per side or until cheese melts and sandwiches are golden brown.

Makes 2 sandwiches

Quick Vegetable & Pesto Salad

¼ cup mayonnaise
¼ cup prepared pesto
1 tablespoon balsamic vinegar
6 cups assorted fresh vegetables from salad bar, such as sliced mushrooms, shredded carrots, red onion strips, sliced radishes, peas, broccoli florets and bell pepper strips (about 1½ pounds)
Lettuce leaves

1. Combine mayonnaise, pesto and vinegar in large bowl; stir until well blended.

2. Add vegetables; toss well to coat. Cover and refrigerate 10 minutes. Arrange lettuce leaves on salad plates. Top with vegetable mixture.

Makes 6 servings

Note: Chilling for 30 minutes will improve the flavor of this easy side-dish salad.

Prep Time: 15 minutes

Sandwiches & Salad

Four-Season Pasta Salad

8 ounces uncooked trumpet-shaped or spiral pasta
1½ cups cauliflower florets
1½ cups sliced carrots
1½ cups snow peas
½ cup Italian or honey-mustard salad dressing

1. Cook pasta according to package directions, adding cauliflower, carrots and snow peas to saucepan during last 3 minutes of cooking time. Drain pasta and vegetables. Place under cold running water to stop cooking; drain again. Transfer to large bowl.

2. Add salad dressing to pasta and vegetable mixture; toss lightly to coat.   *Makes 4 to 6 servings*

Apricot Chicken Sandwiches

6 ounces poached chicken tenders
2 tablespoons apricot fruit spread
2 tablespoons chopped fresh apricots (pits removed)
4 slices whole wheat bread
4 lettuce leaves

1. Drain cooked chicken; chop well. Mix with apricot spread and chopped fruit.

2. Top bread with lettuce leaves. Divide chicken mixture evenly among bread slices; slice in half, folding over to make half-sandwich. Slice each half again to make 2 wedges. Serve immediately.   *Makes 4 servings*

Sandwiches & Salad

Stanley Sandwiches

½ cup shredded carrot
2 tablespoons ranch salad dressing
½ (12-ounce) focaccia bread
3 lettuce leaves
6 ounces thinly sliced deli-style roast beef, roast chicken or roast turkey

Stir together carrot and salad dressing. Cut focaccia into 3 pieces. Split each piece horizontally. Place lettuce leaves on bottom halves. Top with meat. Spoon carrot mixture on top. Top with remaining focaccia halves. Wrap in plastic wrap.　　*Makes 3 servings*

tip: Pack this sandwich in an insulated lunch bag with a frozen water bottle. The sandwich will stay cold and the water will be melted, but nice and cool.

Pear Gorgonzola Melts

4 ounces creamy Gorgonzola cheese (do not use crumbled blue cheese)
8 slices walnut raisin bread
2 pears, cored and sliced
½ cup fresh spinach leaves
   Butter, melted

1. Spread cheese evenly on 4 bread slices; layer with pears and spinach. Top with remaining bread slices. Brush outsides of sandwiches with butter.

2. Place large nonstick skillet over medium heat until hot. Add sandwiches; cook 4 to 5 minutes per side or until cheese melts and sandwiches are golden brown.   *Makes 4 sandwiches*

tip: If Gorgonzola cheese is too strong for you, try this sandwich with Havarti or white Cheddar. The combination with the pear is surprising but delicious.

Main Dish Magic

Beef Teriyaki Stir-Fry

1 boneless beef top sirloin steak (about 1 pound)
½ cup teriyaki marinade and sauce, divided
2 tablespoons vegetable oil, divided
1 medium onion, halved and sliced
2 cups frozen green beans, rinsed and drained

1. Cut beef lengthwise in half, then crosswise into ⅛-inch slices. Combine beef and ¼ cup marinade in medium bowl; set aside.

2. Heat 1½ teaspoons oil in wok or large skillet over medium-high heat until hot. Add onion; stir-fry 3 to 4 minutes or until crisp-tender. Remove from wok to medium bowl.

3. Heat 1½ teaspoons oil in wok. Stir-fry beans 3 minutes or until crisp-tender and hot. Drain off excess liquid. Add beans to onions in bowl.

4. Heat remaining 1 tablespoon oil in wok. Drain beef, discarding marinade. Stir-fry half of beef 2 minutes or until barely pink in center. Remove to bowl. Repeat with remaining beef. Return beef and accumulated juices in bowl to wok. Stir in vegetables and remaining ¼ cup marinade; cook and stir 1 minute or until heated through. Serve with hot cooked rice or noodles.   *Makes 4 servings*

Prep and Cook Time: 22 minutes

5 ingredient cookbook

Main Dish Magic

Buttery Pepper and Citrus Broiled Fish

3 tablespoons MOLLY MCBUTTER® Flavored Sprinkles
1 tablespoon MRS. DASH® Lemon Pepper Blend
1 tablespoon lime juice
2 teaspoons honey
1 pound boneless white fish fillets

Combine first 4 ingredients in small bowl; mix well. Broil fish 6 to 8 inches from heat, turning once. Spread with Lemon Pepper mixture. Broil an additional 4 to 5 minutes.   *Makes 4 servings*

Prep Time: 5 minutes
Cook Time: 10 minutes

Tandoori Chicken Drumsticks

1½ pounds chicken drumsticks
½ cup plain yogurt
4 tablespoons PATAK'S® Tandoori Paste
4 tablespoons chunky-style peanut butter
2 teaspoons cider vinegar

Remove skin from drumsticks and gently score. In large bowl, combine yogurt, tandoori paste, peanut butter and vinegar. Place drumsticks in marinade. Cover and refrigerate at least 1 hour. Grill drumsticks over medium coals 20 to 25 minutes or until cooked through, turning occasionally and basting with remaining sauce.

Makes 4 servings

Main Dish Magic

Cranberry-Glazed Ham

1 (5- to 6-pound) fully cooked spiral sliced ham half*
¾ cup cranberry sauce or cranberry chutney
¼ cup Dijon or hot Dijon mustard
1 teaspoon ground cinnamon
¼ teaspoon ground allspice

*A whole ham is usually 10 to 12 pounds and serves 24. Double glaze ingredients if using a whole ham.

Preheat oven to 300°F. Place ham in large roasting pan lined with heavy-duty aluminum foil. Combine cranberry sauce, mustard, cinnamon and allspice; mix well. Spread half of mixture evenly over top of ham (glaze will melt and spread as it cooks). Bake 1 hour; spread remaining cranberry mixture over top of ham. Continue to bake until internal temperature of ham reaches 140°F, about 1 hour. Transfer ham to carving board; let stand 5 minutes before serving.

Makes 10 to 12 servings

Southwestern Skillet Dinner

1 pound ground beef
2 teaspoons chili powder
1 jar (16 ounces) thick and chunky salsa
1½ cups BIRDS EYE® frozen Corn
¾ cup shredded Cheddar cheese

• Cook ground beef in large skillet over high heat until well browned, about 8 minutes; drain. Stir in chili powder; cook 1 minute.

• Add salsa and corn; bring to boil. Reduce heat to medium; cover and cook 4 minutes.

• Sprinkle with cheese; cover and cook until cheese melts.

Makes about 4 servings

Serving Suggestion: **Serve with rice or tortilla chips. Or, serve as a taco filling.**

Prep Time: 5 minutes
Cook Time: 20 minutes

233

Main Dish
Magic

Mile-High Enchilada Pie

8 (6-inch) corn tortillas
1 jar (12 ounces) salsa
1 can (15½ ounces) kidney beans, rinsed and drained
1 cup shredded cooked chicken
**1 cup shredded Monterey Jack cheese with jalapeño
    peppers**

SLOW COOKER DIRECTIONS

1. Prepare foil handles for slow cooker;* place in slow cooker. Place 1 tortilla on bottom of slow cooker. Top with small amount of salsa, beans, chicken and cheese. Continue layering using remaining ingredients, ending with tortilla and cheese.

2. Cover; cook on LOW 6 to 8 hours or on HIGH 3 to 4 hours. Pull out by foil handles. Garnish with fresh cilantro and slice of red pepper, if desired. *Makes 4 to 6 servings*

*To make foil handles, tear off 18×2-inch strips of heavy foil or use regular foil folded to double thickness. Crisscross foil strips in spoke design and place in slow cooker to make lifting of tortilla stack easier.

Cheesy Sausage and Mushroom Pizza

1 (10-ounce) prepared thin pizza crust (about 12 inches)
½ cup pizza sauce
2 cups (8 ounces) shredded provolone cheese
**8 ounces bulk Italian sausage, cooked, crumbled and
    drained**
1 (4-ounce) can mushroom pieces, drained

Heat oven to 450°F. Spread pizza crust evenly with sauce, 1 cup cheese, sausage, mushroom, and remaining 1 cup of cheese. Bake directly on oven rack for 10 minutes, or until crust is crisp and cheese is melted. *Makes 4 to 5 servings*

Favorite recipe from **National Pork Board**

Main Dish Magic

Grilled Lemon Chicken Dijon

⅓ cup **HOLLAND HOUSE®** White with Lemon Cooking Wine
⅓ cup olive oil
2 tablespoons Dijon mustard
1 teaspoon dried thyme leaves
2 whole chicken breasts, skinned, boned and halved

In shallow baking dish combine cooking wine, oil, mustard and thyme. Add chicken and turn to coat. Cover; marinate in refrigerator for 1 to 2 hours.

Prepare grill for direct cooking. Drain chicken, reserving marinade. Grill chicken over medium coals 12 to 16 minutes or until cooked through, turning once and basting with marinade.*

Makes 4 servings

Do not baste during last 5 minutes of grilling.

Sizzling Florida Shrimp

1½ pounds Florida Shrimp, peeled and deveined
1 cup Florida mushrooms, cut into halves
½ cup Florida red bell pepper pieces (1-inch pieces)
½ cup Florida onion pieces (1-inch pieces)
1 (8.9-ounce) jar lemon pepper sauce or 1 cup barbecue sauce

Arrange shrimp on wooden skewers with mushrooms, red bell pepper and onion. Place skewers in glass dish and cover with sauce, reserving about 2 tablespoons for basting during cooking. Cover and refrigerate for 1 hour. Prepare grill surface by cleaning and coating with oil. Coals are ready when coals are no longer flaming but are covered with gray ash. Place skewers on grill about 6 inches from coals. Grill shrimp for about 3 to 4 minutes on each side, basting with reserved sauce before turning once. Serve with sautéed asparagus and grilled garlic bread. *Makes 4 servings*

Favorite recipe from *Florida Department of Agriculture and Consumer Services, Bureau of Seafood and Aquaculture*

Steamed Maryland Crabs

2 cups water or beer
2 cups cider vinegar or white vinegar
2 dozen live Maryland blue crabs
½ pound seafood seasoning
½ pound salt

1. Place water and vinegar in 10-gallon stockpot. Place steaming rack in bottom of pot. Place half of crabs on rack. Mix seafood seasoning with salt; sprinkle half over crabs.

2. Repeat layering with remaining crabs and seasoning mixture.

3. Cover pot. Cook over high heat until liquid begins to steam. Steam about 25 minutes or until crabs turn red and meat is white. Remove crabs to large serving platter, using tongs.

4. To serve, cover table with disposable paper cloth.

5. To pick crabs, place crab on its back. With thumb or knife point, pry off "apron" flap (the "pull tab"-looking shell in the center) and discard.

6. Lift off top shell and discard.

7. Break off toothed claws and set aside. With knife edge, scrape off 3 areas of lungs and debris over hard semi-transparent membrane covering edible crabmeat.

8. Hold crab at each side; break apart at center. Discard legs. Remove membrane cover with knife, exposing large chunks of meat; remove with fingers or knife.

9. Crack claws with mallet or knife handle to expose meat.

Makes 4 servings

Main Dish Magic

Quick Pasta with Peppers

8 ounces uncooked penne or rigatoni pasta
2 tablespoons olive oil
1 each red, yellow and green bell pepper, thinly sliced
1 jar (26 ounces) marinara sauce
¼ cup grated Parmesan cheese

1. Cook pasta according to package directions; drain.

2. Meanwhile, heat olive oil in large skillet over medium-high heat. Add bell peppers; cook 2 minutes, stirring frequently. Reduce heat to medium-low; stir in marinara sauce. Cook and stir 5 minutes over medium heat, stirring frequently.

3. Pour sauce over hot pasta; sprinkle with cheese before serving.

Makes 6 to 8 servings

57 & Honey Glazed Kabobs

⅔ cup HEINZ 57 Sauce®
⅓ cup honey
4 skinless boneless chicken breast halves, each cut into 8 cubes (about 1 pound)
Fresh vegetables, cut into 1½ inch pieces (such as onions, mushrooms, bell peppers, zucchini and yellow squash)
Cooking spray

Combine 57 Sauce and honey; set aside. Alternately thread chicken and vegetables on skewers. Spray with cooking spray. Grill over medium heat 12 to 15 minutes, turning often, until chicken is cooked. Brush liberally with 57 Sauce mixture. Grill until kabobs are brown and glazed, about 5 minutes.

Makes 4 servings

Main Dish
Magic

Red Snapper Scampi

¼ cup (½ stick) butter, softened
1 tablespoon white wine
1½ teaspoons minced garlic
½ teaspoon grated lemon peel
1½ pounds red snapper, orange roughy or grouper fillets (about 4 to 5 ounces each)

1. Preheat oven to 450°F. Combine butter, wine, garlic and lemon peel in small bowl; stir to blend.

2. Place fish on foil-lined shallow baking pan. Top with seasoned butter. Bake 10 to 12 minutes or until fish begins to flake easily when tested with fork. Season with salt and pepper, if desired.

Makes 4 servings

Tip: Serve fish over mixed salad greens, if desired. Or, add sliced carrots, zucchini and bell pepper cut into matchstick-size strips to the fish in the baking pan for an easy vegetable side dish.

Prep and Cook Time: 12 minutes

tip: Red snapper is firm-textured fish that contains very little fat. It is very versatile and works with almost any cooking method.

Main Dish Magic

Southwestern Enchiladas

1 can (10 ounces) enchilada sauce, divided
2 packages (about 6 ounces each) refrigerated fully-cooked
    steak strips*
4 (8-inch) flour tortillas
1/2 cup condensed nacho cheese soup, undiluted or 1/2 cup
    chile-flavored pasteurized process cheese spread
1 1/2 cups (6 ounces) shredded Mexican cheese blend

Fully cooked steak strips can be found in the refrigerated prepared meats section of the supermarket.

1. Preheat oven to 350°F. Spread half of enchilada sauce in 9-inch glass baking dish; set aside.

2. Place about 3 ounces steak down center of each tortilla. Top with 2 tablespoons cheese soup. Roll up tortillas; place seam side down in baking dish. Pour remaining enchilada sauce evenly over tortillas. Sprinkle with cheese. Bake 20 to 25 minutes or until heated through.   *Makes 4 servings*

Grilled Glazed Salmon

1/3 cup apple juice
2 tablespoons soy sauce
1/2 teaspoon minced fresh ginger
1/8 teaspoon black pepper
1 1/4 pounds salmon fillet

1. Prepare grill for direct grilling. Combine apple juice, soy sauce, ginger and pepper in small saucepan. Bring to a boil over medium heat. Reduce heat; simmer apple juice mixture about 10 minutes or until syrupy. Cool slightly.

2. Brush side of salmon fillet without skin with apple juice mixture. Grill salmon, flesh side down, on oiled grid over medium-hot heat 5 minutes. Turn and brush salmon with apple juice mixture. Grill 5 minutes more or until fish flakes easily when tested with fork.
Makes 4 servings

Main Dish Magic

Steamed Fish Fillets with Black Bean Sauce

1½ pounds white-fleshed fish fillets (Lake Superior whitefish, halibut, rainbow trout or catfish)
1 tablespoon vegetable oil
2 green onions, chopped
2 tablespoons chopped fresh ginger
2 tablespoons black bean sauce*

*Jarred black bean sauce is sold in the Asian food section of most large supermarkets. It is made of fermented black soybeans, soy sauce, garlic, sherry, sesame oil and ginger. Black soybeans have a pungent odor and a unique, pronounced flavor. Do not substitute regular black beans.

1. Fill large saucepan about one-third full with water. Place bamboo steamer basket over saucepan. Or, fill wok fitted with rack about one-third full with water. Cover and bring water to a boil. Place fillets in single layer on platter that fits into steamer or wok.

2. Heat oil in small skillet until hot. Add onions, ginger and black bean sauce; cook, stirring about 30 seconds or just until fragrant. Immediately pour contents of skillet evenly over fillets. Place platter in steamer; cover and steam 10 to 15 minutes or until fish is tender and flaky.

3. Serve fillets and sauce over rice, if desired. Garnish with green onion tops. *Makes 4 servings*

tip: A bamboo steamer basket is a great tool to have in your kitchen. Use it for rice, fish, vegetables, dumplings and much more. You can use virtually no fat, making it a very healthy cooking tool.

Steamed Fish Fillets with Black Bean Sauce

245

Brunch-Time Favorites

Cheddary Sausage Frittata

> **4 eggs**
> **¼ cup milk**
> **1 package (12 ounces) bulk pork breakfast sausage**
> **1 poblano pepper,* seeded and chopped**
> **1 cup (4 ounces) shredded Cheddar cheese**

*Poblano peppers can sting and irritate the skin, so wear rubber gloves when handling peppers and do not touch your eyes.

1. Preheat broiler.

2. Combine eggs and milk in medium bowl; whisk until well blended. Set aside.

3. Heat 12-inch ovenproof nonstick skillet over medium-high heat until hot. Add sausage; cook and stir 4 minutes or until no longer pink, breaking up sausage with spoon. Drain sausage on paper towels; set aside.

4. Add pepper to same skillet; cook and stir 2 minutes or until crisp-tender. Return sausage to skillet. Add egg mixture; stir until blended. Cover; cook over medium-low heat 10 minutes or until eggs are almost set.

5. Sprinkle cheese over frittata; broil 2 minutes or until cheese is melted. Cut into 4 wedges. Serve immediately.   *Makes 4 servings*

Smart Tip: If skillet is not ovenproof, wrap handle in heavy-duty aluminum foil.

5 ingredient cookbook

Brunch-Time Favorites

Banana Roll-Ups

¼ cup smooth or crunchy almond butter
2 tablespoons mini chocolate chips
1 to 2 tablespoons milk
1 (8-inch) whole wheat flour tortilla
1 large banana, peeled

1. Combine almond butter, chocolate chips and 1 tablespoon milk in medium microwavable bowl. Microwave on MEDIUM (50%) 40 seconds. Stir well and repeat if necessary to melt chocolate. Add more milk if necessary for desired consistency.

2. Spread almond butter mixture on tortilla. Place banana on one side of tortilla and roll up tightly. With sharp knife, cut into 8 (1-inch) slices.

Makes 4 servings

Zucchini-Orange Bread

1 package (about 17 ounces) cranberry-orange muffin mix
1½ cups shredded zucchini (about 6 ounces)
1 cup water
1 teaspoon ground cinnamon
1 teaspoon freshly grated orange peel

1. Preheat oven to 350°F. Grease 8×4-inch loaf pan; set aside.

2. Combine muffin mix, zucchini, water, cinnamon and orange peel in medium bowl; stir just until dry ingredients are moistened. Spoon batter into prepared loaf pan; bake 40 minutes or until toothpick inserted into center comes out almost clean.

3. Cool in pan on wire rack 5 minutes. Remove bread from pan to wire rack; cool completely. Serve plain or with cream cheese, if desired.

Makes about 16 slices

Brunch-Time Favorites

Maple Mix Dip

1 package (4-serving size) cook and serve vanilla pudding mix
2 cups milk
⅓ cup maple syrup, divided
¼ teaspoon ground cinnamon
Assorted dippers, such as mini waffles, graham crackers, vanilla wafer cookies, apple slices and/or pear slices

1. Stir pudding mix, milk, 2 tablespoons maple syrup and cinnamon in medium saucepan over medium heat. Cook and stir until mixture simmers and thickens. Divide mixture evenly between 4 small bowls or custard cups.

2. Divide remaining syrup between 4 bowls, drizzling over pudding surface. Allow cups to cool to lukewarm before serving. Serve with assorted dippers, such as mini waffles, graham crackers, wafer cookies, apple slices or pear slices, if desired.

Makes 4 to 6 servings

Sticky Buns

24 frozen bread dough rolls, thawed
1 package (4-serving size) cook-and-serve butterscotch pudding and pie filling mix (not instant)
½ cup firmly packed brown sugar
½ cup chopped pecans
½ cup (1 stick) butter, melted

1. Grease 12-cup Bundt pan. Layer rolls in pan. Sprinkle pudding mix, brown sugar and pecans over rolls. Drizzle butter on top. Cover pan with foil and refrigerate overnight.

2. Preheat oven to 400°F. Remove foil and bake 20 minutes or until lightly browned. Invert rolls onto serving plate. *Makes 24 servings*

Tip: Place a baking sheet underneath Bundt pan while baking to catch drippings.

Brunch-Time Favorites

Apple and Cheese Pockets

2 medium to large Golden Delicious apples, peeled, cored and finely chopped (2 cups)
2 cups shredded sharp Cheddar cheese
2 tablespoons apple jelly
¼ teaspoon curry powder
1 package (16 ounces) refrigerated large biscuits (8 biscuits)

1. Preheat oven to 350°F. Line baking sheet with parchment paper; set aside.

2. Combine apples, cheese, apple jelly and curry powder in large bowl and stir well.

3. Roll out each biscuit on lightly floured board to 6½-inch circle. Place ½ cup apple mixture in center. Fold biscuit over filling to form a semicircle; press to seal tightly. Place on baking sheet. Bake 15 to 18 minutes or until biscuits are golden and filling is hot.

4. Reheat leftover pockets in microwave about 30 seconds on HIGH until hot. *Makes 8 servings*

Note: Refrigerate leftovers up to two days or freeze up to one month.

Brunch-Time Favorites

Cinnamon Chip Filled Crescents

2 cans (8 ounces each) refrigerated quick crescent dinner rolls
2 tablespoons butter or margarine, melted
1⅔ cups (10-ounce package) HERSHEY'S Cinnamon Chips, divided
Cinnamon Chips Drizzle (recipe follows)

1. Heat oven to 375°F. Unroll dough; separate into 16 triangles.

2. Spread melted butter on each triangle. Sprinkle 1 cup cinnamon chips evenly over triangles; gently press chips into dough. Roll from shortest side of triangle to opposite point. Place, point side down, on ungreased cookie sheet; curve into crescent shape.

3. Bake 8 to 10 minutes or until golden brown. Drizzle with Cinnamon Chips Drizzle. Serve warm. *Makes 16 crescents*

Cinnamon Chips Drizzle: Place remaining ⅔ cup chips and 1½ teaspoons shortening (do not use butter, margarine, spread or oil) in small microwave-safe bowl. Microwave at HIGH (100%) 1 minute; stir until chips are melted.

Crab Bagel Spread

4 ounces cream cheese, softened
2 ounces crabmeat, shredded
2 tablespoons chopped green onion tops
4 teaspoons lemon juice
1 tablespoon milk

Beat cream cheese in small bowl on medium speed of electric mixer until smooth. Add remaining ingredients; mix until well blended. Refrigerate until ready to serve. Serve with bagels, toast or crackers, if desired. *Makes about ¾ cup*

Leek Frittata

6 eggs
¾ cup milk
1 package KNORR® Recipe Classics™ Leek recipe mix
1 tablespoon vegetable oil
½ cup shredded Cheddar cheese (2 ounces)

• In medium bowl, with wire whisk, beat eggs and milk until smooth; stir in recipe mix.

• In large nonstick skillet, heat oil over medium heat. Add egg mixture and immediately reduce heat to low. Cover and cook 3 minutes.

• Uncover, stir well and sprinkle with cheese. Cover and cook 3 minutes longer. Let stand covered 5 minutes.

Makes 3 to 4 servings

Prep Time: 15 minutes

Creamy Citrus Fruit Dip

¼ cup vanilla yogurt
2 teaspoons lemon juice
2 teaspoons sugar
¼ teaspoon vanilla
1 cup honeydew or cantaloupe cubes

In a small bowl, combine all ingredients, except melon. Stir until well blended. Serve with melon.

Makes 2 servings

Brunch-Time Favorites

Twice Baked Cheddar Ham Potatoes

6 medium baking potatoes, unpeeled and baked
1 jar (1 pound) RAGÚ® Cheesy! Double Cheddar Sauce
1 cup frozen green peas, thawed
¼ pound ham steak, chopped
¼ cup shredded cheddar cheese (about 1 ounce)

Preheat oven to 400°F.

Cut a lengthwise slice from top of each potato. Scoop pulp from each potato leaving ½-inch-thick shells; set aside. In medium bowl, mash pulp, then stir in Double Cheddar Sauce, peas and ham. Evenly fill potato shells with potato mixture.

On baking sheet, arrange stuffed potatoes and bake 15 minutes. Sprinkle with cheese and bake an additional 5 minutes or until heated through.
Makes 6 servings

Prep Time: 15 minutes
Cook Time: 20 minutes

tip: A baked potato is like a blank canvas. Set up your favorite toppings next to the baked potatoes and let everyone make their own. Baked potato bar will always be a hit!

Brunch-Time Favorites

Smoked Salmon Hash Browns

3 cups frozen hash brown potatoes, thawed
2 pouches (3 ounces each) smoked Pacific salmon*
½ cup chopped onion
½ cup chopped bell pepper
2 tablespoons vegetable oil

*Smoked salmon in foil packages can be found in the canned fish section of the supermarket. Do not substitute lox or other fresh smoked salmon.

1. Combine potatoes, salmon, onion and bell pepper in bowl; toss gently to mix well.

2. Heat oil in large nonstick skillet over medium-high heat. Add potato mixture; spread to cover surface of skillet. Carefully pat down to avoid oil spatter.

3. Cook 5 minutes or until crisp and browned. Turn over in large pieces. Cook 2 to 3 minutes or until brown. Season with salt and pepper. *Makes 4 servings*

Popovers

3 eggs
1 cup milk
1 tablespoon butter, melted
1 cup all-purpose flour
¼ teaspoon salt

1. Preheat oven to 375°F. Grease 12 standard (2½-inch) muffin cups or 6 custard cups.

2. Beat eggs, milk and butter in medium bowl. Add flour and salt; beat until smooth. Pour batter into prepared cups, filling about three-fourths full. (If using custard cups, place on baking sheet.) Bake 45 to 50 minutes or until brown and crispy. Serve immediately.
Makes 12 small or 6 large popovers

Cheese Popovers: Add ⅛ teaspoon garlic powder and ¼ cup grated Parmesan cheese to batter. Bake as above.

Brunch-Time Favorites

Quick Breakfast Sandwiches

2 breakfast sausage patties
3 eggs
2 teaspoons butter
2 whole wheat English muffins, split and toasted
2 slices Cheddar cheese

1. Cook sausage according to package directions; set aside and keep warm.

2. Beat eggs in small bowl. Melt butter in small skillet. Pour in eggs; cook and stir gently over low heat until just set. Season eggs with salt and pepper to taste.

3. Place cheese on bottom halves of English muffins; top with sausage and scrambled eggs. Serve immediately.

Makes 2 sandwiches

Tip: Sausage breakfast patties may vary in size. If patties are small, use two patties for each sandwich.

Asparagus Frittata Casserole

3 large eggs
1½ cups 1% milk
1 teaspoon salt
1 box (10 ounces) BIRDS EYE® frozen Deluxe Asparagus Spears, thawed
½ cup shredded Monterey Jack or Cheddar cheese

• Preheat oven to 400°F.

• In medium bowl, beat eggs. Add milk and salt; blend well.

• Pour mixture into greased 9×9-inch baking pan; top with asparagus.

• Sprinkle with cheese.

• Bake 15 minutes or until egg mixture is set.

Makes 4 servings

Prep Time: 5 minutes
Cook Time: 15 minutes

So-Sweet Endings

Banana Oatmeal Caramel Cookies

1 package (18 ounces) refrigerated turtle cookie dough
2 ripe bananas, mashed
1⅓ cups uncooked old-fashioned oats
⅔ cup all-purpose flour
½ cup semisweet chocolate chips

1. Let dough stand at room temperature about 15 minutes. Preheat oven to 350°F. Lightly grease cookie sheets.

2. Combine dough, bananas, oats and flour in large bowl; beat until well blended. Drop dough by heaping tablespoonfuls 2 inches apart onto prepared cookie sheets; flatten slightly.

3. Bake 16 to 18 minutes or until edges are brown and centers are set. Cool on cookie sheets 1 minute. Remove to wire racks; cool completely.

4. Place chocolate chips in small resealable food storage bag. Microwave on MEDIUM (50%) 1 minute; knead bag lightly. Microwave and knead at additional 30-second intervals until chocolate is completely melted. Cut off tiny corner of bag. Drizzle melted chocolate over cookies. Let stand until set.

Makes about 2 dozen cookies

Variation: Use triple chocolate cookie dough instead of the turtle dough.

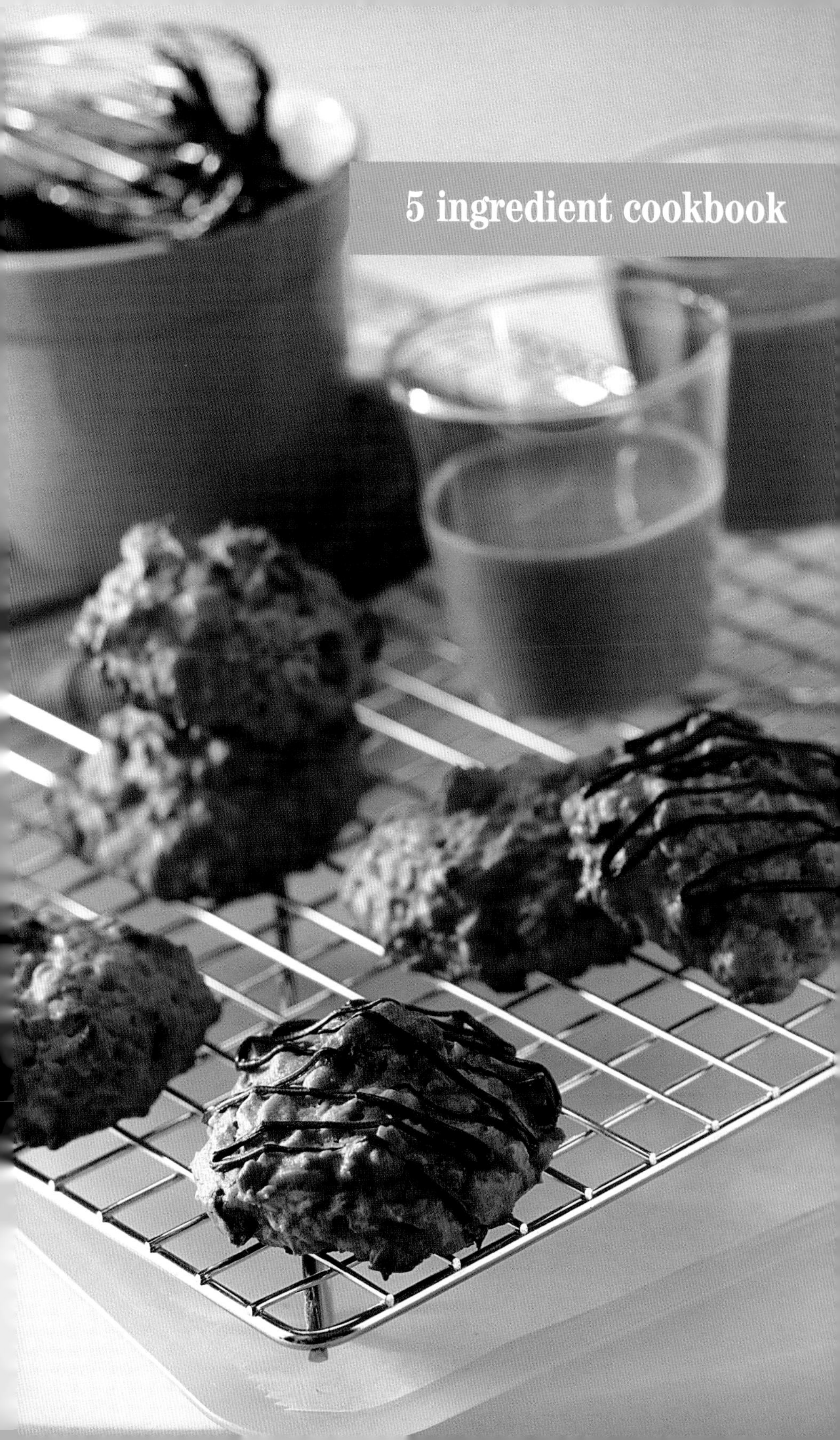
5 ingredient cookbook

Rocky Road Candy

2 cups (12 ounces) semisweet chocolate chips
2 tablespoons butter or margarine
1 (14-ounce) can EAGLE BRAND® Sweetened Condensed
**   Milk (NOT evaporated milk)**
2 cups dry-roasted peanuts
1 (10½-ounce) package miniature marshmallows

1. Line 13×9-inch baking pan with wax paper. In heavy saucepan, over low heat, melt chocolate chips and butter with EAGLE BRAND®; remove from heat.

2. In large bowl, combine peanuts and marshmallows; stir in chocolate mixture. Spread in prepared pan. Chill 2 hours or until firm.

3. Remove candy from pan; peel off paper and cut into squares. Store loosely covered at room temperature.

Makes about 3½ dozen candies

Microwave method: In 1-quart glass measure, combine chocolate chips, butter and EAGLE BRAND®. Cook at HIGH (100% power) 3 minutes, stirring after 1½ minutes. Stir to melt chips. Let stand 5 minutes. Proceed as directed above.

Prep Time: 10 minutes
Chill Time: 2 hours

So-Sweet Endings

S'More Bars

1 package (18 ounces) refrigerated chocolate chip cookie dough
¼ cup graham cracker crumbs
3 cups mini marshmallows
½ cup semisweet or milk chocolate chips
2 teaspoons shortening

1. Let dough stand at room temperature about 15 minutes. Preheat oven to 350°F. Grease 13×9-inch baking pan. Press dough into prepared pan. Sprinkle evenly with graham cracker crumbs.

2. Bake 10 to 12 minutes or until edges are golden brown. Sprinkle with marshmallows. Bake 2 to 3 minutes or until marshmallows are puffed. Cool completely in pan on wire rack.

3. Combine chocolate chips and shortening in small resealable food storage bag; seal. Microwave on HIGH 1 minute; knead bag lightly. Microwave on HIGH for additional 30-second intervals until chips and shortening are completely melted and smooth, kneading bag after each 30-second interval. Cut off small corner of bag. Drizzle over bars. Refrigerate 5 to 10 minutes or until chocolate is set. Cut into bars. *Makes 3 dozen bars*

tip: Don't be impatient when melting chocolate. Follow the instructions above or you could end up burning the chocolate.

Chocolate Almond Sandwiches

1 package (18 ounces) refrigerated sugar cookie dough
4 ounces almond paste
¼ cup all-purpose flour
1 container (16 ounces) dark chocolate frosting
Sliced almonds

1. Let dough stand at room temperature about 15 minutes.

2. Combine dough, almond paste and flour in large bowl; beat until well blended. Divide dough into 3 pieces; freeze 20 minutes. On waxed paper or plastic wrap, shape each piece into 10×1-inch log. Wrap tightly in plastic wrap; refrigerate at least 2 hours or overnight. (Or freeze about 1 hour or until firm.)

3. Preheat oven to 350°F. Lightly grease cookie sheets. Cut dough into ⅜-inch slices; place 2 inches apart on prepared cookie sheets.

4. Bake 10 to 12 minutes or until edges are light brown. Cool 2 minutes on cookie sheets. Remove to wire racks; cool completely.

5. Spread scant 2 teaspoons frosting each on bottoms of half the cookies; top with remaining cookies. Place dab of frosting and sliced almond on top of each sandwich cookie.

Makes about 2½ dozen sandwich cookies

Note: Almond paste is a prepared product made of ground blanched almonds, sugar and an ingredient, such as glucose, glycerin or corn syrup, to keep it pliable. It is often used to as an ingredient in confections and baked goods. Almond paste is available in cans and plastic tubes in most supermarkets or gourmet food markets. After opening, wrap the container tightly and store it in the refrigerator.

So-Sweet Endings

Mini Chocolate Cheesecakes

8 squares (1 ounce each) semisweet baking chocolate
3 packages (8 ounces each) cream cheese, softened
½ cup sugar
3 eggs
1 teaspoon vanilla

1. Preheat oven to 325°F. Lightly grease 12 standard (2½-inch) muffin pan cups; set aside.

2. Place chocolate in 1-cup microwavable bowl. Microwave on HIGH 1 to 1½ minutes or until chocolate is melted, stirring after 1 minute. Let cool slightly.

3. Beat cream cheese and sugar in large bowl with electric mixer at medium speed about 2 minutes or until light and fluffy. Add eggs and vanilla; beat about 2 minutes or until well blended. Beat melted chocolate into cream cheese mixture until well blended.

4. Divide mixture evenly among prepared muffin cups. Place muffin pan in larger baking pan; place on oven rack. Pour warm water into larger pan to depth of ½ to 1 inch. Bake cheesecakes 30 minutes or until edges are dry and centers are almost set. Remove muffin pan from water. Cool cheesecakes completely in muffin pan on wire rack.

Makes 12 cheesecakes

Mini Swirl Cheesecakes: Before adding chocolate to cream cheese mixture, place about 2 heaping tablespoons of mixture in each muffin cup. Add chocolate to remaining cream cheese mixture in bowl; beat until well blended. Spoon chocolate mixture on top of plain mixture in muffin cups. Swirl with knife before baking.

Heavenly Chocolate Mousse Pie

**1 (14-ounce) can EAGLE BRAND® Sweetened Condensed Milk
(NOT evaporated milk)**
4 (1-ounce) squares unsweetened chocolate, melted
1½ teaspoons vanilla extract
1 cup (½ pint) whipping cream, whipped
1 (8-inch) prepared chocolate or graham cracker crumb crust

1. In medium bowl, beat EAGLE BRAND®, melted chocolate and vanilla until well blended.

2. Chill 15 minutes or until cooled; stir until smooth. Fold in whipped cream.

3. Pour into crust. Chill thoroughly. Garnish as desired. Store leftovers covered in refrigerator. *Makes 1 (8-inch) pie*

Prep Time: 20 minutes

Fudgy Banana Rocky Road Clusters

1 package (12 ounces) semisweet chocolate chips
⅓ cup peanut butter
3 cups miniature marshmallows
1 cup unsalted peanuts
1 cup banana chips

1. Line baking sheets with waxed paper. Grease waxed paper.

2. Place chocolate chips and peanut butter in large microwavable bowl. Microwave on HIGH 2 minutes or until chips are melted and mixture is smooth, stirring twice. Fold in marshmallows, peanuts and banana chips.

3. Drop rounded tablespoonfuls of candy mixture onto prepared baking sheets; refrigerate until firm. Store in airtight container in refrigerator. *Makes 2½ to 3 dozen clusters*

Tip: If you prefer more nuts, use chunky peanut butter.

So-Sweet Endings

Tiny Hot Fudge Sundae Cups

1 package (18 ounces) refrigerated sugar cookie dough
⅓ cup unsweetened cocoa powder
5 to 7 cups vanilla ice cream
Hot fudge ice cream topping, colored sprinkles and aerosol whipped cream
9 maraschino cherries, cut into quarters

1. Let dough stand at room temperature about 15 minutes. Preheat oven to 350°F. Spray 36 mini (1¾-inch) muffin pan cups with nonstick cooking spray.

2. Combine dough and cocoa in large bowl; beat until well blended. Divide dough into 36 equal pieces; shape each piece over outside of prepared muffin pan cup. Bake 10 to 12 minutes or until set. Cool on pans 10 minutes. Remove cups from pans; cool completely on wire racks.

3. Fill each cooled cookie cup with 2 to 3 tablespoons ice cream. Drizzle with hot fudge sauce; top with sprinkles. Garnish each sundae cup with whipped cream and cherry quarter.

Makes 3 dozen sundae cups

tip: Mix this recipe up with different flavors of cookie dough or ice cream. Replace the sprinkles with chopped nuts for adults.

Easy Holiday Shortbread Cookies

1 cup (2 sticks) unsalted butter, softened
½ cup powdered sugar
2 tablespoons packed light brown sugar
¼ teaspoon salt
2 cups all-purpose flour

1. Beat butter, sugars and salt in large bowl with electric mixer on medium speed 2 minutes or until light and fluffy. Add flour, ½ cup at a time, beating well after each addition.

2. Form dough into ball; shape into 14-inch log. Wrap log tightly in plastic wrap. Refrigerate 1 hour.

3. Preheat oven to 300°F. Cut log into ½-inch-thick slices; place on ungreased cookie sheets. Bake 20 to 25 minutes or until lightly browned. Cool 5 minutes on cookie sheets. Remove to wire racks to cool completely.   *Makes 28 cookies*

Note: Dough can be stored in the refrigerator up to two days, or in the freezer for up to one month. If frozen, thaw the dough log in the refrigerator overnight before slicing and baking.

So-Sweet Endings

Chocolate Crunchies

1 package (18 ounces) refrigerated sugar cookie dough
½ cup unsweetened cocoa powder
1 egg
½ teaspoon ground cinnamon
3 bars (1.55 ounces each) milk chocolate with crisp rice candy, chopped

1. Let dough stand at room temperature about 15 minutes. Preheat oven to 350°F. Lightly grease cookie sheets.

2. Combine dough, cocoa, egg and cinnamon in large bowl; beat until well blended. Stir in candy. Shape dough into ¾-inch balls; place 2 inches apart on prepared cookie sheets.

3. Bake 7 to 9 minutes or until set. Cool on cookie sheets 1 minute. Remove to wire racks; cool completely.   *Makes about 3 dozen cookies*

Cheesecake-Filled Strawberries

1 package (8 ounces) cream cheese, softened
1½ tablespoons powdered sugar
1½ teaspoons vanilla
1 pint strawberries
1 package (8 ounces) sliced almonds, toasted

1. Beat cream cheese 2 to 3 minutes in medium bowl with electric mixer at medium speed. Add powdered sugar and vanilla; beat until well blended.

2. Trim and discard stem ends from strawberries. Scoop out pulp, leaving ¼-inch shell; fill with cream cheese mixture. Top each strawberry with 2 toasted almonds.

3. Place strawberries on serving plate. Refrigerate until ready to serve.
Makes 4 to 6 servings

Tip: The strawberries can also be filled by cutting a wedge out of the side of each berry and scooping out the pulp, leaving about a ¼-inch shell. Fill the strawberries and arrange as desired.

Peanut Butter Truffles

2 cups (11½ ounces) milk chocolate chips
½ cup whipping cream
2 tablespoons butter
½ cup creamy peanut butter
¾ cup finely chopped peanuts

1. Combine chocolate chips, whipping cream and butter in heavy, medium saucepan; melt over low heat, stirring occasionally. Add peanut butter; stir until blended. Pour into pie pan. Refrigerate about 1 hour or until mixture is fudgy but soft, stirring occasionally.

2. Shape mixture by tablespoonfuls into 1¼-inch balls; place on waxed paper.

3. Place peanuts in shallow bowl. Roll balls in peanuts; place in petit four or paper candy cups. (If peanuts won't stick because truffle has set, roll truffle between palms until outside is soft.)

4. Truffles can be refrigerated 2 to 3 days or frozen several weeks.

Makes about 36 truffles

Tip: For a pretty contrast, roll some of the truffles in cocoa powder instead of chopped peanuts.

Acknowledgments

The publisher would like to thank the companies listed below for the use of their recipes in this publication.

ACH Food Companies, Inc.

Alouette® Cheese, Chavrie® Cheese, Saladena®

BelGioioso Cheese, Inc.

Birds Eye Foods

Cabot® Creamery Cooperative

Chef Paul Prudhomme's Magic Seasoning Blends®

Del Monte Corporation

EAGLE BRAND®

Florida Department of Agriculture and Consumer Services, Bureau of Seafood and Aquaculture

Heinz North America

The Hershey Company

The Hidden Valley® Food Products Company

Hillshire Farm®

Holland House® is a registered trademark of Mott's, LLP

Hormel Foods, LLC

Jennie-O Turkey Store®

JOLLY TIME® Pop Corn

The Kingsford® Products Co.

Mrs. Dash®

National Pork Board

National Watermelon Promotion Board

North Dakota Wheat Commission

Ortega®, A Division of B&G Foods, Inc.

Perdue Farms Incorporated

Reckitt Benckiser Inc.

Stonyfield Farm®

Reprinted with permission of Sunkist Growers, Inc. All Rights Reserved.

Unilever

Washington Apple Commission

Index

Index

Index

Index

Index

Index

METRIC CONVERSION CHART

VOLUME MEASUREMENTS (dry)

$1/8$ teaspoon = 0.5 mL
$1/4$ teaspoon = 1 mL
$1/2$ teaspoon = 2 mL
$3/4$ teaspoon = 4 mL
1 teaspoon = 5 mL
1 tablespoon = 15 mL
2 tablespoons = 30 mL
$1/4$ cup = 60 mL
$1/3$ cup = 75 mL
$1/2$ cup = 125 mL
$2/3$ cup = 150 mL
$3/4$ cup = 175 mL
1 cup = 250 mL
2 cups = 1 pint = 500 mL
3 cups = 750 mL
4 cups = 1 quart = 1 L

VOLUME MEASUREMENTS (fluid)

1 fluid ounce (2 tablespoons) = 30 mL
4 fluid ounces ($1/2$ cup) = 125 mL
8 fluid ounces (1 cup) = 250 mL
12 fluid ounces ($1 1/2$ cups) = 375 mL
16 fluid ounces (2 cups) = 500 mL

WEIGHTS (mass)

$1/2$ ounce = 15 g
1 ounce = 30 g
3 ounces = 90 g
4 ounces = 120 g
8 ounces = 225 g
10 ounces = 285 g
12 ounces = 360 g
16 ounces = 1 pound = 450 g

DIMENSIONS

$1/16$ inch = 2 mm
$1/8$ inch = 3 mm
$1/4$ inch = 6 mm
$1/2$ inch = 1.5 cm
$3/4$ inch = 2 cm
1 inch = 2.5 cm

OVEN TEMPERATURES

250°F = 120°C
275°F = 140°C
300°F = 150°C
325°F = 160°C
350°F = 180°C
375°F = 190°C
400°F = 200°C
425°F = 220°C
450°F = 230°C

BAKING PAN SIZES

Utensil	Size in Inches/Quarts	Metric Volume	Size in Centimeters
Baking or	$8 \times 8 \times 2$	2 L	$20 \times 20 \times 5$
Cake Pan	$9 \times 9 \times 2$	2.5 L	$23 \times 23 \times 5$
(square or	$12 \times 8 \times 2$	3 L	$30 \times 20 \times 5$
rectangular)	$13 \times 9 \times 2$	3.5 L	$33 \times 23 \times 5$
Loaf Pan	$8 \times 4 \times 3$	1.5 L	$20 \times 10 \times 7$
	$9 \times 5 \times 3$	2 L	$23 \times 13 \times 7$
Round Layer	$8 \times 1 1/2$	1.2 L	20×4
Cake Pan	$9 \times 1 1/2$	1.5 L	23×4
Pie Plate	$8 \times 1 1/4$	750 mL	20×3
	$9 \times 1 1/4$	1 L	23×3
Baking Dish	1 quart	1 L	—
or Casserole	$1 1/2$ quart	1.5 L	—
	2 quart	2 L	—